Squared Away

Squared Away

How Can Bankers Succeed as Economic First Responders

By:

Jeff Marsico

Wolf Moon Publishing Company

Elizabethtown, Pennsylvania

Published by Wolf Moon Publishing Company, Elizabethtown, Pennsylvania

Edited by Kate Young

Library of Congress:

ISBN: 978-0-9826938-2-7

About the Author

 How do you answer "who wrote this" in a couple paragraphs? How can you capture the thought process of what went into this book? Jeff Marsico grew up one of three high-spirited boys to a widowed mother in Scranton, Pennsylvania, where he played baseball in the summer, basketball in the winter, and caused trouble in between. Nobody had the heart to tell him he was good at neither sport. He knew he was good at trouble. Although there was little history of a college education in his family, and even less money for him to go, he went anyway. But had to come up with the funds to do it. So he got his first banking job in 1985 making microfiche during second shift in the basement of a community bank. Not satisfied with the slow progress, he joined the greatest Navy in the world with an eye to serve because all of his preceding generations did so. But he also had a goal of completing his education. He did, but not without sacrifice, as he spent days (and sometimes consecutive months) serving his country as a cryptologist, and nights with his Tandy 286 computer doing schoolwork. Since leaving the Navy, Jeff has served in branch management and as an internal consultant for a regional bank helping to consolidate merged banks. From that launching point, he began his 20+ year consulting career exclusively serving financial institutions where he specializes in strategy development, profit and process improvement, performance measurement, and financial advisory. He has moderated and executed hundreds of financial institution strategy assignments and has advised on mergers totaling over $2.5 billion in market value. His wife was his high school sweetheart, and his daughters are his most awesome achievement. He is the author of the banking blog, Jeff For Banks (www.jeff4banks.com). His author page can be found at www.jeffmarsico.com.

"Business is good because it creates value, it is ethical because it is based on voluntary exchange, it is noble because it can elevate our existence, and it is heroic because it lifts people out of poverty and creates prosperity."

John Mackay and Raj Sisodia from *Conscious Capitalism*

Contents

Introduction

C ommunity financial institutions are economic first responders. That's not just my opinion. FDIC Chairman Jelena McWilliams made that point at an industry event. It was a recognition of how important the United States' version of banking is to the success of the economy. The truth of this was laid bare during the pandemic, when the U.S. Treasury turned to financial institutions to quickly distribute aid to small businesses suffering uncertainty and significant decline in revenues.

The challenge is that, as you read this, our ecosystem of diverse financial institutions of different sizes, missions, and areas of expertise is being culled. Rapidly. By approximately 4 percent per year, net of start-up banks, or de novos. Banks—and even credit unions—continue to merge, with little de novo activity to offset the decline. In 1990, there were more than 15,000 FDIC-insured financial institutions. At the time of writing, only one third of that total remained. In 2005, the 10 largest financial institutions owned 43 percent of total industry assets. In 2019, they owned 52 percent.

Why the decline? Are we over-banked? Is technological change happening too fast? Do we need greater scale to drive down the cost of regulation? According to a 2014 study, non-depository financial institutions and depository financial institutions—i.e., the banking system—ranked fourth and fifth respectively in terms of most-regulated industries.[i]

The answer is probably a mix of all of the above. And I would add one other critical element: a challenged business model.

At publicly traded financial institutions, a focus on generating shareholder value at the expense of other stakeholders leads to short-term thinking. And that comes at the expense of long-term strategy—which, eventually, leads to shareholder disappointment over multiple periods. Frequently, this is what triggers a sale. Operating quarter-to-quarter is a sure sign of a business that rarely makes the strategic investments to fuel innovation and its next level of growth.

At financial institutions that are shareholder owned but not publicly traded, it's a neglect of shareholders that often results in a sale. Meanwhile, at non-shareholder owned institutions, acquisition is often rooted in a lack of operating discipline. Shareholders demand accountability. Without an accountable operating discipline, resources are easily misallocated. And that stunts growth by limiting the strategic investments that offer the most promise for future profit generation.

What's the solution? I think it's imperative for financial institutions to build the kind of culture, strategies, and execution they need to be relevant—even vitally important—to their stakeholders. Those are the institutions that have earned their right to remain independent. And, if a merger is in the cards, those are the institutions that can take it on from a position of strength. Not from a position of weakness, irrelevance, and backward thinking. *Squared Away* was written for those seeking cultural and operating discipline to be the financial institutions that are strong and earned their right to remain independent.

Readers can implement ideas specific to their own institutions. Ideas on how to allocate resources more efficiently—and how to equally serve all primary stakeholders: customers, employees, communities, and shareholders (if applicable). Why? Because those stakeholders are interdependent. Balancing their needs increases the likelihood of long-term success for all of them. Create an institution where employees enjoy coming to work and have a sense of serving a higher purpose. In turn, customers get great and distinguishable service from happy, committed employees. Loyal, satisfied customers—along with a strong operating discipline—enable the kind of long-term performance that generates shareholder value. A high-value institution has resources available, and can target them toward initiatives that make a community impact. All of these elements work together to build a strong brand—one that's indispensable to its community—which further benefits all stakeholders. And it becomes a self-perpetuating cycle.

That said, I will not tell readers they "must do" this, or "have to do" that. Each institution's situation is different. It would be presumptuous for me to assume I know each and every one of your situations and prescribe the implementation of any one idea. Consider this an opportunity to learn what has worked at other banks and to think about how that might fit with your circumstances.

Readers will find philosophical similarities to the 2014 book *Conscious Capitalism* by Raj Sisodia and Whole Foods Market co-founder John Mackey.[ii] In fact, I considered "Conscious Banking" as a potential title for this work. But this book and that one do not fall into lockstep. In fact, I did not stumble upon that gem of a book until I had written about 75 percent of this one.

The place where the two books align is the idea that the next iteration of capitalism can be far greater than predecessor versions. Also:

the hypothesis that dutifully serving all primary stakeholders can lead to better outcomes. I would go on to say that for financial institutions, one of those "better outcomes" is earning the right to remain independent. If your institution builds the operating discipline to serve all of its stakeholders, why would employees want to work anywhere else? Why would customers want to bank anywhere else? What communities wouldn't benefit from having your institution in it? And what other stock would shareholders prefer to own?

Curated by Readers

This book, unlike most others, was curated by readers. What I mean by that is, when choosing topics to include in the book, I looked to what readers of my blog, Jeff for Banks (www.Jeff4Banks.com), read the most.

For the past 10 years I have been writing articles for community financial institution leaders. At first, I did this for selfish reasons. To improve my writing skills. To research micro issues to help me be better at my profession. And to provide a forum to exchange ideas with other bankers and those who serve them. As the readership grew, I learned a lot about what readers wanted most to read.

So the banking topics covered in this book are driven by the top 20 most-read articles. These articles are included within each chapter, in their original form, set off by the "∞" symbol. Some chapters include multiple articles related to a particular topic or theme. However, the work published on my blog tells only part of the story. With each chapter, I introduce additional concepts, facts, and ideas for readers to consider. The articles guided the subject matter, but did not limit the chapter's depth or breadth.

About This Book

This book has been over 35 years in the making. It is informed by a banking career that began when I was hired at the age of 19 to make microfiche in the basement of a Scranton-based community financial institution. It draws on lessons learned during my years as a cryptologist in the U.S. Navy. It was there that I learned about leadership, strategy, and the power of investing in employee development. The Navy invested plenty in me, so I know firsthand the difference that can make on many levels. For the past 20 years, I've been a consultant to the banking industry. In that role, my biggest challenge has been moderating strategy development with a thought to a financial institution's aspirational future. Management teams have been culturally acclimated to think no further than next year's budget. In some cases, next quarter's earnings. We must evolve.

This book tells a cohesive story, so it's best consumed from beginning to end. However, readers can also pick and choose chapters that most interest them, and circle back to other chapters later. Although the concepts do build, one on top of another, I was mindful of readers who prefer to browse according to their own needs.

The topics within the book are broken into four sections:

If you take the pick-and-choose approach, consider doing so by section, as each chapter builds upon its predecessor within each section. Note: If you're with a financial institution that is not shareholder owned, do not discount the section on creating a valuable institution. That information applies to you too. After all, nobody wants an institutional epithet that reads, "Here lies ABC Bank. Meh." The value of your financial institution is crucial to all of your stakeholders, not just shareholders.

I also suggest reading with a notepad handy. Write down topics and approaches that you might want to pursue further. As I mentioned, this book is not meant to preach to you, as everyone's situation is different. But consider sketching out a menu of ideas that you can take back to your financial institution. Use it as food for thought on ways to build a culture of operating discipline. Think about how your institution's resources can be directed to the most promising products, lines of business, and stakeholders.

Holdouts

Inevitably, there will be those who doubt the need to change. The rapidly shrinking number of financial institutions is not enough to convince them that they need to evolve into something that may be materially different from what they are now. Can you get by with only slight changes to business as usual? Or do you need to overhaul your thinking, culture, strategy, and execution?

Here's one way to look at it: The present value of your institution's strategy should be close to what the institution could reasonably achieve in a sale. The difference between those numbers is the strategy value gap. Does your institution calculate that figure? It measures whether shareholders would be better off if your bank were acquired. Managing that gap will be an important component in serving all of your stakeholders. Your board might tolerate a larger gap if you are truly meaningful to your employees, customers, and communities. Do you matter?

If you are still a holdout, ask yourself whether branches are important to your strategy. If so, how many open branch positions are filled by support center employees who voluntarily post to go into the branch? In my experience, employees prefer to flow the other way. They flee branches for the better work hours and pay in support positions. They flee branches to get away from customers. This is symptomatic of a financial institution's misplaced priorities, employee development, and incentives. It's the hallmark of a culture that needs attention. If a bank is serving a higher purpose, and balancing its commitment to all stakeholders, employees should be knocking down doors to be in front of customers.

An institution that has happy, well-developed employees delivering a differentiated experience to customers—while improving the plight of its communities and delivering solid returns to shareholders—is one built to last. You can be that institution.

Section I

People First

Rare is the financial institution that does not consider employees as critical to its success. Even rarer is the financial institution that actually acts like employees are critical to its success.

Chapter 1

Build the Foundation: Keep the Keepers

Financial institutions serve four primary stakeholders: employees, customers, shareholders, and communities. Not necessarily in that order. But what is the appropriate order? Where do employees belong on your list?

That depends on your strategy. Perhaps digital delivery of banking services—with a heavy dollop of highly efficient artificial intelligence—keeps your costs so low that your bank can afford to entice customers with price. Maybe in that case, heavily proceduralized, easy-to-execute processes that require little skill might allow you to put employees at the lower end of your constituency list. Turnover would need to remain manageable, of course, and the time and effort to train new employees would have to be minimal.

But that is not a scenario I often hear about in bank strategy sessions. As you will glean across the course of this book, price-driven growth is not highly valued by bank stock investors. They prefer much harder stuff. And regardless of whether your financial institution is publicly traded, you can learn important lessons from the people who place a value on banks every day. After all, those are the folks who take the broadest view of what it takes to make a bank succeed.

And the "harder stuff" that bank investors are looking for? That, as

I've come to learn, centers on a bank's ability to build relationships, core deposit growth, net interest margin management, expense discipline, skilled management, and promising markets. Growth by price—combined with expense discipline—might yield above-average profits. But it won't necessarily earn the respect or the valuations of the buyers and sellers of bank stocks. Operating discipline can. And that's different from expense discipline alone.

The harder stuff requires relationship builders, technology enablers, change champions, and people motivators. In other words, it requires a talented and motivated employee base that shares the bank's vision and can harness resources to achieve it. It requires the acquisition and retention of what I call The Keepers.

My original look at the topic provides a jumping-off point.

∞

Employee Retention: Keep the Keepers

March 2, 2019

https://www.jeff4banks.com/2019/03/employee-retention-keep-keepers.html

You have a highly valued employee, and they quit. Why? The boss? The culture? The pay?

I'm sure if I searched for credible sources, I would get some version of one or a combination of the three. It is highly individualized. But what is universal is that each financial institution has employees that are

highly valued and they want to keep. Yet rarely tell them so. For fear that the employee will recognize their worth and ask for more money or shop themselves around. Better to repress that employee, right? Shhhh. Don't say a thing.

The most recent Bureau of Labor Statistics analysis shows the number of quits, i.e. employee-driven departures, at 3.5 million in December 2018, the highest since pre-recession 2007.

Best Strategy

The best single strategy for employee retention is management attention, according to Bill Conerly, a business economist and former banker.[iii] Employees may tell you they are leaving for more money, and if your compensation is not in the ballpark for the value they can get on the open market, then perhaps that is true. But if comp is in the ballpark, then it is likely the employee wouldn't be looking around if the company's culture was great and their boss paid attention to them.

Management and leadership are soft skills that are not on a financial institution's priority list. Seven years ago I wrote about this on these pages, and I haven't seen much improvement since. In that post, I wrote of a former military commander that worked for a large corporation that incorporated leadership into their development program. They hired psychologists to develop the curriculum, and actors to role play.

So, in addition to the ideas below, it is important for financial institutions to develop good managers with leadership abilities. Because they are the ones that will be executing the following ideas to retain your high performers.

Three Ideas to Improve Retention

1. **Build a culture that salutes achievement.** Accountability shouldn't be based on fear, recrimination, and public flogging. It should be built on open recognition of a job well done. Be it exceeding goals, achieving top quartile profitability, most improved, or proposing and implementing an innovative idea. Give that employee a trophy. Coach under-achievers that have an attitude of self-improvement. Because, as one of my Navy Senior Chiefs once told me, if you have an employee that puts forth the effort and has a good attitude, and they don't succeed, that's on the supervisor.

2. **Set career paths.** And develop employees to achieve. So many financial institution development programs are ad hoc. No direction. But if you hire a junior credit analyst out of college, once they get the job, ask them what they aspire to be. Aside from compliance and functional training, develop them to hit their next level. Even if it is outside of Credit. Perhaps they want to be a commercial lender and some day, be CEO of your bank. That's great! If they achieve within their functional position, then we should be prepared to develop them for the next level. Instead of pushing them down in their current position because they are really good at it. Which is a sure fire way to have them shopping their resume, in my opinion.

3. **Conduct stay interviews.** Now, I will admit that I'm cynical about buzzwords. But I received a newsletter from a financial institution executive recruiter that caught my eye on improving

employee engagement. Stay interviews will help your financial institution make tweaks to its culture and employee relations, and improve employee engagement, which I hear is a key reason why high performing employees stay. Because they matter to you.

During our most recent podcast, we answered listener questions and one question was "what is the most effective way to recruit and find talent in a community bank?" My answer, build from within.

Because there aren't many employees out on the street. And to woo them, you might have to pay up. And if you pay up, you may run into "equal pay" movements happening in many states, pricing up your existing talent. An unintended consequence.

What would you rather do to build an employee base capable of executing your strategy? Buy or build?

~ Jeff

∞

I can think of no better way to start a book on banking in general, and community banking in particular, than to talk about the people who make your bank run. Without the right people in place, all the best practices become hypothetical. So let's dig more deeply into those three steps to employee retention and development.

Salute Achievement

The idea of puffing up the egos of your team members may run contrary to your DNA. At least it does mine. Appropriately recognizing and celebrating success, however, is a critical discipline for those who lead others. Based on my observation, it is common to err on the side of pointing out mistakes and shortcomings. Some supervisors feel the need to make themselves appear superior or more knowledgeable; others criticize their staff because that is how they were supervised. They need to fix mistakes, therefore they point out mistakes. That approach can be a trap, though, as unrelenting nit-picking tends to deflate and demotivate employees.

To create a culture in which employees are consistently motivated toward success, financial institutions should get serious about leadership development. Unfortunately, from what I've seen, leadership development is not routinely offered to employees at community financial institutions. This may be why we see so many cases of the Peter Principle playing out—where staffers are promoted to the point of ineffectiveness. An experienced, reliable, proficient loan servicing employee, for example, does not automatically make for an excellent loan servicing supervisor. There's an enormous difference between being responsible for your own performance and being responsible for the performance of others under your charge.

Knowing how to maximize the abilities of a staff is a learned skill. Do you rely on your employees to know this and to seek out instruction on their own? Is your bank's culture so strong—and are your hiring practices so thorough—that employees self-motivate and don't need the supervisor to help maximize their talent? Maybe so. But I doubt it.

My own experience with leadership development is rooted in my military training. Front and center to that was a two-week curriculum on how to motivate sailors under my charge. It was called NAVLEAD. (There's an acronym for everything in the military.) But even with military training, my evolution as a leader and manager needed refinement. And it came from the most unexpected place.

I was picking up my daughter, then age 12, from a lacrosse camp hosted by the local athletic association. The camp was a success, and when it ended, the athletic association proposed joining the area middle-school league. The catch: they needed volunteer coaches. I'm still not sure how it happened—perhaps all other parents took one step backwards—but at the end of that camp I was the middle school girls' lacrosse coach.

I'd never played lacrosse. Even if I had, boys' and girls' lacrosse are different. Worse, I'd never even seen a lacrosse game. What I had seen were terrible coaches up and down youth sports. And I've got news for you: it's terrible, even through the college ranks.

I recently read about the Texas Tech women's basketball program, whose coach created an environment described by players as one of "fear, anxiety and depression."[iv] Coaches are an extreme form of supervisor: Performance feedback is immediate. Emotions run high. But, like the head of loan servicing, they are responsible for getting those under their charge to maximize their abilities. Do you think using heart monitor readings to shame players into an extreme state of exertion is appropriate? Reportedly, some do. In both banking and sports, team motivation is critical, but so are boundaries.

One coach who's figured out a constructive technique is former

NFL standout, author, and coaching expert Joe Ehrmann, author of *Inside Out Coaching: How Sports Can Transform Lives*. When I landed the girls' lacrosse coach position, I immersed myself in books and videos like this.

In addition, the athletic association sent me to a coaching camp—where I thought I was going to learn girls' lacrosse. And I did. But part of that curriculum was the Positive Coach, a program administered by the not-for-profit Positive Coaching Alliance. I thought, "What is this? I need to learn girls' lacrosse, not how to be a coach." How wrong I was.

One concept of the training is the "magic ratio." In order to fill a player's emotional tank, your feedback to a player should be five positive comments to one negative. Five to one! I don't know where you grew up, or what coaches you've had in the past, but if I got one to five, I'd consider myself lucky.

But the key is this: if you provide authentic praise for something a player does right, and do so in front of the other players, when it comes time to correct something, you will have greater credibility and the player will be open to the constructive criticism. This won't be the case if all you do is criticize. What type of environment are you creating if players fear feedback from their coach? How will they trust you if it's always negative, 100 percent of the time? According to PCA's research, to maximize player talent, the magic ratio is the effective way to do it. This is consistent with Ehrmann's philosophy.

Has anyone taught you—or any of your employees who are now supervising others—about the magic ratio? Because the concept applies. If we want to create an environment where employees maximize their abilities, we need to fill their emotional tanks. We need to salute them for a job well done far more than we criticize them for mistakes.

Leadership and supervision are learned skills. They must be taught. Is it part of your employee development?

Set Career Paths

Chris Collingsworth, an NBC sportscaster covering past Olympics, reported that Apolo Ohno trained four times a day, for two hours each session. Ohno, as many of you know, was a U.S. short-track speed skater. His events might take two minutes to complete. He trained eight hours a day.

Now consider your bank's strategic planning session. Suppose that in it, your bank identifies the aspiration to become the top consumer bank in your markets by advising customers on how to improve their net worth. Great! Now, turn and look at the employees you expect to execute on such an aspiration. Can they do it?

If they can't, what are you doing to give them the tools to succeed? What career paths are they pursuing? It is here, in the realm of employee development, that I see the biggest gap between strategic aspiration and ability to execute on it. Time and time again, I ask bank executives and human resources professionals about career paths and employee development, and I hear crickets.

 In the Navy, I rode several ships, and while at sea we constantly trained for war. Aside from specific job training, those ships had an all-encompassing training regimen that taught each enlisted sailor all facets of ship operations so they'd be prepared to step into a number of roles in combat. This training culminated in the awarding of the Enlisted

Surface Warfare Specialist (ESWS, pronounced EE-swas). Wearing that pin (see image) signified you were a highly trained surface warrior…Navy elite.

What kind of training can banks use to give their employees not just a basic level of competence, but also an upward ladder defined by bank strategy? Right now, so much of the typical bank's training budget is dedicated to compliance and operations. It's focused on mandatory things, while all other training is implemented in an ad hoc fashion, if at all. That creates a shortfall for developing the kind of training programs designed to propel the bank toward achieving its strategic goals.

If your bank aims to be the best in service, for example, think of the service standards set by giants in the hospitality industry, like Ritz-Carlton hotels. What are your exact service standards—and how are you training staff to achieve them? If you aspire to be an advisor, the same question stands. What training have you implemented to create a staff of advisers who exemplify your brand promise?

I once led the training department in a 200-person division at Navy Field Station, Kunia, Hawaii. For every person in that division—to help them become proficient in their current job and the next step up—we had a spreadsheet, much like the one pictured below.

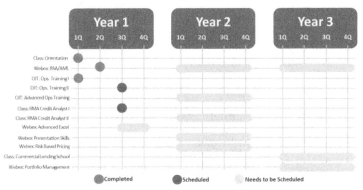

Imagine how appreciated your top performers feel when you not only train them to excel in their current position, but you also begin developing them for their next one. Say you have a branch banker who is doing well, has talent, and dreams of becoming a commercial lender. In discussing their career path within your organization, should you crush their dreams to prevent the branch from losing them? I've got news for you: they would go anyway. Find their career path within your bank and be their resource for making it happen. Keepers are keepers. Hoard them at the bank level, not your department.

Conduct Stay Interviews

In my original article, I touched on the value of conducting "stay interviews"—that is, periodically checking in with employees, one-on-one, to discuss opportunities and concerns, and ultimately decrease attrition. Although the concept may sound trendy, it's really an expression of a well-established approach to employee retention. Because, beyond recognition and training, a third crucial way to keep the keepers is to give your employees a voice and make them feel like business partners.

Marcel Schwantes, CEO of training firm Leadership From the Core, has written about Acuity, a property/casualty insurer that gives employees a voice in directing the company's annual charitable donations. Along with Acuity's other employee engagement initiatives, this has led to an astonishingly low voluntary turnover rate of 2 percent.[v] Quite the antidote for concerns that investing in employee career paths is wasted on people who might eventually depart, wouldn't you say?

When you give employees a voice, be prepared for what you might hear and be ready to act on it. For example, if you've built a rapport and open communication with your staff, you'll learn, as I have, that one thing that irritates keepers is tolerance of slackers. In fact, if you never hear any grumbling about low performers, then I suggest your communication may not be as open as you think.

Low performers are like anchors. Not only do they push work onto those around them, but they also drag down the performance of top performers. This is especially true at banks whose compensation philosophy is a 3 percent raise to top performers and 2 percent for the bottom. Why should staff bother trying? You wind up dragging keepers down to a level of mediocrity. And if that doesn't happen, your best employees will leave because you've created an environment tolerant of poor performance, with insignificant reward for those who excel. Your stay interviews will "out" the low hanging fruit pretty quickly. And you would be surprised at how morale improves with a strategic firing.

Think of the stay interview as a tool for an organization that learns. One that wants to hone its craft. One that constantly seeks improvement and values the input of all employees in making that happen. You want to keep the keepers? Give them a voice.

At the beginning of this chapter I said your strategy should be your guidepost in determining the keepers. It is worth noting that banking is changing at a faster pace than it has in the past, particularly with digital adoption. Although I don't consider myself a futurist who can predict your institution's demise if you don't adopt a particular technology, I am an evolutionist. And the personnel who complement the technology at your bank should be evolving with the times.

When identifying the keepers, think of those who will challenge processes and look for a way to automate them. Think of those who can extract data from your systems in a meaningful way to identify your most profitable customers, alert relationship managers to opportunities, and automatically notify customers about suspicious activity or savings and borrowing opportunities. Think of those who can maximize the systems you already have, or find new systems to move you forward.

Give your employees the opportunity to evolve into the new "keepers." But regardless of whether they are current or future employees, we have to move forward to build an enduring future.

To Sum It Up…

Your most valuable assets go up and down the elevator every day. Not all employees are alike. You have all-stars, reliable team players, and low performers. They are easy to identify, but if your employee evaluation system works, then they are likely broken down numerically. This chapter focused on the all-stars, or the "keepers." But there is also value in those reliable team players. In order to keep those employees who will move your bank forward, succeed in executing your strategy, and deliver value to your customers and other stakeholders, you need to purposefully implement a plan to partner with keepers and align your bank's success with their success.

Points Made This Chapter

❖ Keepers should be identified by their ability to execute your strategy, or the "harder stuff."

❖ The best single strategy for employee retention is management attention.

❖ If you have an employee who has a good attitude and puts forth the effort yet doesn't succeed, that's on you.

❖ The magic ratio—five positive feedback interactions for every one negative—fills an employee's emotional tank and helps them maximize their abilities.

❖ Don't fear losing keepers to other departments. Fear losing them to other banks. Setting their career paths and becoming a partner in achieving their goals reduces this risk.

❖ Make employees partners in your department's and bank's success. Give them a voice. Empower them.

❖ A strategic firing can improve morale.

❖ If you believe that your most valuable assets are the ones that go up and down the elevator every day, do something about it.

❖ Realize that the skills needed to move your bank forward may be very different from those that worked in the past.

Chapter 2

Culture Building in a Telecommuting World

You might think I first took on the topic of telecommuting amidst the global pandemic and the flood of workers moving from their offices to their guest bedrooms. But you would be wrong. Who would've thought, when I wrote the original article in January 2019, that 16 months later 42 percent of Americans would telecommute?[vi]

❖ There is a wider issue beyond the technical do's and don'ts of telecommuting. Companies in every industry need to grapple with the M-word—motivation—and C-word—culture. How do you build them when new hires are starting from home? How do you nurture them when a third of your staff is not in the office? How do you change them when you don't see your long-timers every day?

❖ Before we entered the 2020 pandemic, telecommuting was on the rise, but represented well below 10 percent of the work force. Extraordinary events brought on its meteoric ascent, and we can expect the pendulum to swing back downward. But not to pre-pandemic levels. So we need to build on what we're learning along the way.

Our perceptions about who can telecommute and what functions can be done in a home office have been challenged. The general observation is that a significant proportion of banking can be done from home. Because, like it or not, the shift happened. But not in the neatly tied box that we expected.

Instead of coming to the broad stroke conclusion that one whole department or another can productively work at home, we've found that some people, in some functions, are well suited for work-at-home, while some others, performing the same functions, are not. According to Stanford Institute for Economic Policy Research, only 51 percent of people working from home felt they did so at 80 percent capacity or greater.[vii]

Before going deeper, here is what I wrote about it.

∞

IMO: How to Make Telecommuting Work in Banks

January 19, 2019

https://www.jeff4banks.com/2019/01/imo-how-to-make-telecommuting-work-in.html

Schlepping to the office five days a week is enough to make employees, or would be employees, reconsider working for you. This is

particularly true in urban areas, where 20 miles might equal an hour commute. Or in growing families, where daycare costs might eat their pay check. In comes telecommuting.

And in an era of high competition for top-notch employees, even stick in-the-mud old schoolers have to consider telecommuting as an option for employees. Currently, there are an estimated 3.9 million telecommuters in the US. Up 115% from 2005.

How To Manage It?

Jane has a 20 mile commute and bears a high proportion of parental duties, and works two days a week from home. Seems fair.

John, her coworker performing in a similar job, is denied telecommuting. John doesn't have parental responsibilities. His commute is about the same as Jane.

Mana from heaven for discrimination lawyers.

So you give in to John so he doesn't call the law offices of Duey, Cheatem, and Howe. You give him a laptop and set him up at home.

Later, you have to reprimand John for his lack of availability while working from home. He promptly quits. And has your laptop. With your customers' information on it. Safely in John's spare bedroom, where he now uses it to play Grand Theft Auto (GFA).

Imagine that disclosure to your customers? "Your personal information may have been compromised to a Missouri teen that achieved Level 20 on Grand Theft Auto and somehow gained access to one of our laptops in the possession of a former disgruntled employee that was playing GFA with the alleged data thief."

So what should you do? I have ideas. Most came from the ABA Banking Journal's thought provoking podcast: How to Make Telework Work in a Bank.[viii]

Making it Work

1. **Have a policy.** In order to avoid discrimination and missing

half of your department, develop a policy that all telecommuting decisions are made from. For example, the policy may read "after two years of continuous employment, a manager may grant permission for an employee to work from home either temporarily or on some routine schedule, depending on the circumstances." And then spell out the decision map that the manager must follow. Like exceptions to loan policy, there may be exceptions to this policy. Such as waiving the two-year requirement for competitive reasons (if the new employee had telecommuting as part of their prior employers benefits). But have as specific a policy as possible to make it clear when telecommuting is permissible to minimize gray areas, discrimination, employee envy, and dissatisfaction.

2. **Use Virtual Desktops.** Solutions such as Citrix or Horizon transforms static desktops into secure, digital workspaces that can be delivered on demand. Meaning a telecommuter can use a VDI app to access their at-work desktop as if they were actually at work. And since the VDI is only delivering images of their desktop, data is not stored on the computer in their home. This solves for systems security and patching. And if the employee leaves, like our doppelganger John above, no worries. Access can be turned off from HQ.

3. **Set expectations clearly.** The ABA podcast suggested signing a contract with the employee. Such as ensuring they work a regular workday, instead of setting their own hours. You don't

want branch staff calling a telecommuting employee for an IRA minimum required distribution amount and that person be out food shopping because the crowds are lighter at the supermarket mid afternoon. And be clear on days in the office versus working from home. Even if the telecommuting contract is short term, such as an employee recouping from a broken femur suffered while skiing.

4. **Use office chat software.** Such as HipChat or Slack. You may not have the "shout over the cubicle" capability with the telecommuter, but you can almost have it with an office chat application. They are getting such wide acceptance, they are being used instead of shouting over the cubicle. So why not take advantage of technology?

5. **Use video to include telecommuters in meetings.** A risk of telecommuting is that this valuable employee, that you thought so valuable that you allow to work from home, would be disconnected to the workforce. Phone calls are one thing. But doubling up on the connectivity with video will improve internal camaraderie and make at-work and telecommuting employees feel more connected. If it means they have to shower and get out of their pajamas, so be it.

My millennial daughter recently asked an employer if she could telecommute a couple of days per week. The company said they were just implementing a new policy to accommodate that. So if you are a telecommuting resister, it's coming whether you like it or not.

I hope you can use the above ideas to make it work.

What other ideas do you have?

~ Jeff

∞

"Have a policy" and "set expectations clearly" might imply rigid rules, hours, and production. The more rigid you are, the less motivated the employee. I would suggest setting guardrails instead of ironclad walls. Allow employees leeway in making it work for them, with enough room to experiment on what works and doesn't work. We should accept that this might be different for different people. This, of course, could increase discriminatory risk, or "legal risk" in bank regulatory and risk appetite parlance. But creating an inflexible, one-size-fits-all solution increases the risk that you can't experiment and make adjustments—which is so important to organizational learning. In other words, it increases the operational risk that telecommuting might fail at your institution.

Returning to the concepts of motivation and culture, consider these two main strategic risks of telecommuting—and how to avoid letting them ultimately lead to increased operational risk.

Motivation

Have you heard that working remotely equates to remotely working? There is an adjustment to be made. If you have difficulty, as I do, sitting in front of a workstation for more than an hour without a mental break or change of pace, you tend to drift out of your work area and grab a coffee, chat with a coworker, or check the news. When at work, the distractions can be short, unless they are related to other work. And there is always the pressure, hopefully internal pressure, to get back at it. Because everyone around you is working.

At home, not so much. Taking that five-to-ten minute respite from work could result in fixing a light, walking the dog, or taking a nap. Why was the *Seinfeld* episode in which George Costanza built a bed under his desk so funny? Because we've all thought about the work nap. When working from home, without the soft peer pressure of our hard-working colleagues, that nap can be a reality.

According to a study performed by Vega Factor, an organizational consultancy, motivation decreases for telecommuters—especially if telecommuting was not their choice.[ix] Why would that be? The authors identified three positive motivators that fall into jeopardy when employees are working from home.

Play. Odd choice of words, perhaps, but this refers to the joys of being in the office with someone. At my firm, we play office golf. The loser of the round gets the Elton, a trophy with Elton John's picture on it. Can't explain why. Just believe me when I say we try to avoid the Elton. But play isn't limited to games. What about the chatter over the cubicle on making a recommendation to eliminate a process without increasing risk? You bounce it off a couple of colleagues to get a feel for the possible objections before proposing it to the boss. With your coworkers on board, you then make the recommendation and receive a well-done from the boss. That feeling is priceless. Whether it's work-related play or just plain old horsing around, how do you replace it to keep your telecommuters motivated?

Purpose. I just interviewed a seasoned banker who made a passionate case for mentoring. She believes a mentor is a sort of safety net for the more junior employee, providing the comfort of judgment-free conversation if the junior employee is struggling at work. But more than that, she believes that mentorship benefits the mentor as well. Because it gives the mentor purpose. A sense they are helping a fellow human being. That there is someone who values their input. Aside from mentorship, think about how else office employees experience purpose in their work that telecommuters may be missing out on. Because we all want our work to be meaningful. To keep telecommuters motivated, give them purpose. This includes pursuing a higher purpose for your institution.

Potential. Out-of-sight-out-of-mind can be a dangerous place for employees. All other things being equal, would a boss be more inclined to coach the in-office employee or the telecommuter to maximize their potential? Even if location bias is not the reality, the telecommuter might perceive it that way. Because the fact is, their onsite counterparts have greater access to the boss, colleagues and neighboring departments. To keep employees motivated, supervisors should be particularly mindful of this perception, and make sure they communicate to the telecommuter that they are just as interested in maximizing their potential, investing in their development, and advancing their career path as the office worker.

Culture

Culture, as I would define it, is the unwritten set of boundaries that your bank operates under—the compass that drives decision making, even when executives or supervisors are not the ones deciding. Meaning that, when a branch manager or a teller makes a judgment decision, they do so in the context of your bank's culture.

Your aspirational culture can be documented. And we often see this in strategic plan values statements. But a written description of the culture you are trying to create is meaningless if your leaders don't consistently practice it, hold people (including themselves) accountable to it, and align policies, procedures, and incentives to be consistent with it. Your telecommuting policy—and how it is executed—should be no different.

When I hear bankers talk reflectively about their culture, I often see disconnects. For example:

- ❖ I rarely hear bankers tell me that their culture is about "production, production, production." But I often see lender incentives based on production. Is your culture about price? Because the easiest way to drive production is through price.

- ❖ I have never heard a banker say they want a culture of customer relationships driven by offering unsuitable products. Yet it is not uncommon to see branch bankers incentivized on number of accounts opened, or the oft-cited open/close ratio. Consider how Wells Fargo's draconian quota system led to a massive cultural disconnect.

- ❖ I rarely hear bankers say they want a culture of fear and recrimination, but it is not unusual to see support centers evaluated on the number of audit exceptions.

Don't create cultural disconnects when developing and implementing your telecommuting policy. Because many of your workers will in fact be telecommuting, consider taking the opportunity to perform a cultural gap analysis between the culture you want and the one you have. Even if it bruises your ego.

Most bankers want an accountability culture. My ideas on how to build one flow out of the last chapter's discussion on filling the employees' "emotional tanks." Here are five suggestions for how you can build an accountability culture that will help motivate telecommuters and office workers alike.

1. **Make accountabilities measurable and transparent.** When I was a branch manager in the mid '90s, our sales incentive system was called RAISE (Realizing Achievement in Sales Excellence). I could calculate my quarterly bonus to the penny. I ran a spreadsheet before spreadsheets were cool. Another branch manager and I used to bet a beer each quarter on the size of our bonus. It worked. The best performers got the highest bonuses. Although RAISE could have been improved to include customer suitability to reduce the risk of a quota system, it was nonetheless measurable and transparent.

2. **Link to your strategy.** Precious few banks state that their strategy is to rely on very tight pricing to close deals on large commercial real estate loans. Yet they continue to measure lender success by dollar production and portfolio size, incentivizing them to do just that. Instead, look to your strategy when building incentive systems.

3. **Have a little friendly competition.** As previously mentioned,

my branch manager friend and I created our own internal competition that ended in a beer at the end of every quarter. It was fun and motivated us to excel. I didn't want to show up for that meeting getting my butt kicked by my friend. Who would? Why not create ranking reports that include multiple measures, such as lender ROE, branch profitability (both ratio and dollars), or best trends in support center productivity? Be careful to not use punishment avoidance as the motivator, like the Texas Tech basketball coach who used heart monitors to gauge player exertion (see last chapter). Be thoughtful about how you implement. Make sure that guardrails are consistent with your strategy and the culture you are trying to create.

4. **Include support centers.** Everyone thinks: if only those branches were squared away, all would be well. So we prune the branch network, and branch staffing, etc. But how about all of those people in compliance or audit? How are they performing? It is understandably more difficult to evaluate support staff because we are not measuring their profitability. However, we can use trends and benchmarks to highlight highly productive support centers and personnel and reward them appropriately, regardless of whether their desk is in the office or at home.

5. **Have an awards ceremony.** I once was in Nashville the week of the CMA Awards. What a production! Entertainers tend to award themselves a lot. So why can't bankers? Imagine having a ceremony that celebrates your "Most Improved Branch," or

"Top ROE Lender," or "Most Productive Support Unit." Imagine your own awards ceremony, one that creates a positive environment, promotes friendly internal competition, and provides peer recognition for a job well done.

The key is to include telecommuters as equal participants in your culture. Put in the extra effort to include them. Take advantage of the telecommuting trend to evaluate and, if necessary, reset your culture to be the bank you want to be. The bank that employees want to work for is likely to also be the one where customers prefer to bank.

To Sum It Up...

The narrow challenge of telecommuting becomes much broader when you go from 5 percent of your workforce to 25 percent. The guardrails you create to facilitate this trend will impact your entire bank. How your financial institution maintains its culture in this emerging environment assumes you have a culture worth maintaining. With change comes opportunity. Bankers who want to create a motivated workforce with a positive accountability culture—a place where people want to work—should consider how they implement their telecommuting policy. This will inform how they manage and motivate all employees, whether they are in the office or at home.

Points Made This Chapter

❖ Nearly half of the U.S. workforce telecommuted during the pandemic, and that number is not likely to ever return to pre-pandemic levels. Telecommuting is here to stay.

❖ Some people, in some functions, can thrive as telecommuters. However, not every job function, and not every employee, is well suited for it.

❖ Guardrails, rather than rigid rules, are needed for telecommuting. Each eligible employee should have enough flexibility to make it work within the organization's needs.

❖ Not having rigid policies and procedures for telecommuters might increase legal risk. However, it will reduce operational risk, as the ability to try different approaches to help home office workers succeed will foster organizational learning.

❖ Banks can motivate telecommuters by replacing or replicating their ability to "play," giving them purpose, and maximizing their potential. Motivation does not need to depend on where the employee's desk is.

❖ Use the telecommuting trend as an opportunity to perform a culture gap analysis. Describe the culture you want and determine if it's the culture you have. Fill the gap.

❖ The dramatic change in how work gets done gives bankers the opportunity to create a positive accountability culture to maximize potential and create an environment where employees want to work.

Chapter 3

What Makes an Effective Community

Banking Board?

Is there a correlation between a bank board's composition and the institution's financial performance? If so, what's the secret sauce?

Across ten years of publishing on banking topics, my research in this area has drawn more readers than any of the other 400 banking stories I've covered.

It's worth noting, this inquiry was my second look at board composition. In my first attempt, I focused on the board members' professions at the nation's top- and bottom-performing financial institutions, as measured by return on equity (ROE). Although it seems high performing financial institutions tend to have attorneys on their boards, I found no definitive theme.

So in this second foray, I look at the professional backgrounds and ages of board members, as well as the size of the board. And instead of focusing on ROE as the yardstick for performance, I've selected the top and bottom performers in terms of total return to shareholders, a method I analyze annually.

Here's what I wrote about it.

∞

What Makes an Effective Community Banking Board?

January 12, 2019

https://www.jeff4banks.com/2019/01/what-makes-effective-community-banking.html

Frequently asked. Seldom answered.

According to the FDIC, directors' responsibilities include:

"Directors are responsible for selecting, monitoring, and evaluating competent management; establishing business strategies and policies; monitoring and assessing the progress of business operations; establishing and monitoring adherence to policies and procedures required by statute, regulation, and principles of safety and soundness; and for making business decisions on the basis of fully informed and meaningful deliberation."[x]

Capiche?

So how do you, as an executive or Chair of your financial institution, construct your Board to be the most effective at the above and delivering solid shareholder returns? Over two years ago, I analyzed this same question, using top five and bottom five Return on Equity banks. I could find no correlation between professional backgrounds of board members and bank performance.

You may have read last month's Top 5 in Total Return to Shareholders[xi] post, where I searched for the best financial institutions in delivering long-term value to shareholders. The average 5-year total return for this group was 320%. Do their boards share something in common that other boards do not? See for yourself.

Carolina Financial Corporation		
Position	**Age**	**Profession**
Chairman	55	Equity Investor
CEO	57	Banker
Board	51	Consultant/Former Banker
Board	69	Accountant/Retired
Board	67	Banker/Retired
Board	54	Advertising
Board	46	Manufacturing
Board	75	Attorney
Board	63	Physician
Board	63	Retain Home Furnishings
Board	70	Attorney
Board	66	Construction/Restoration
Board	74	Mortgage Banking/Retired
Board	66	Architect
Board Size: 14	Average Age: 63	

Oregon Bancorp, Inc.		
Position	**Age**	**Profession**
Chairman	78	Banker/Retired
Vice Chair	65	Accountant
CEO	64	Banker
Board	61	Construction/Commercial
Board	65	Ag Supply
Board	57	Sand/Gravel Supply
Board	67	Automotive Aftermarket/Retired
Board	56	Heavy Duty Parts
Board	63	Nursery/Wholesale
Board Size: 9	Average Age: 64	

Farmers & Merchants Bancorp, Inc.		
Position	**Age**	**Profession**
Chairman	65	Retail Clothing
Vice Chairman	68	Retail Furniture/Retired
CEO	68	Banker
Board	65	Fertilizer and Seed
Board	63	Accountant
Board	64	Trucking
Board	56	Academia
Board	58	Farming
Board	57	Woodworking

Board	65	Professor
Board Size: 10	Average Age: 63	

Fidelity D&D Bancorp, Inc.		
Position	**Age**	**Profession**
Chairman	65	Attorney
Vice Chairman	63	Attorney
CEO	52	Banker
Board	68	Real Estate Brokerage
Board	70	Conultant/Retired
Board	85	Educator/Retired
Board	48	Uniform Supply
Board	81	Consultant/Retired Banker
Board	84	Uniform Supply/Retired
Board Size: 9	Average Age: 68	

Plumas Bancorp		
Position	**Age**	**Profession**
Chairman	65	Water and Timber Companies
Vice Chairman	74	Forestry/Retired
CEO	53	Banker
Board	64	Real Estate Broker, Farming
Board	78	Banker/Retired
Board	75	Forest Products Wholesale
Board	70	Banker/Retired

Board	60	Accountant
Board Size: 8	Average Age: 67	

The average board size was 10, and the average age was 65. The average number of bankers, active or retired, was two to three. Remember that we are including the CEO, who is also on the Board.

So, what about the Bottom 5 in Total Return to Shareholders? Recall from the Top 5 post that I screened for low trading volume banks. So those with less than 1,000 shares traded per-day were removed. The average 5-year total return for the group below was -31%.

Here is the board composition of those on the unenviable Bottom 5 list.

Bancorp, Inc.		
Position	**Age**	**Profession**
Chairman	48	Investment Firm/Bank Employee
Vice Chairman	60	Asset Management/Former Bank Employee
CEO	53	Banker
Board	51	Investment Firm
Board	73	Healthcare Services/ Former Banker
Board	71	Private Equity/ Former Banker
Board	70	Attorney
Board	77	Attorney/ Former Judge

Board	60	Investment Firm
Board	51	Investment Banker
Board Size: 10	Average Age: 61	

Carver Bancorp, Inc.		
Position	**Age**	**Profession**
Chairman	70	Retired Banker
CEO	47	Banker
Board	71	Government/Retired
Board	68	Bank Regulator/Retired
Board	87	Retired Banker
Board	70	Real Estate Investor/ Retired CFO of Tribe
Board	55	Investment Banker
Board	56	Entertainment/Media
Board	66	Asset Management
Board	65	Community Development
Board Size: 10	Average Age: 66	

MidSouth Bancorp, Inc.		
Position	**Age**	**Profession**
Chairman	44	Horse Breeder/Retired NFL QB
Vice Chairman	60	Retired Banker
CEO	59	Banker
Board	67	Real Estate Investor

Board	80	Private Investor
Board	61	Physician
Board	65	Private Equity
Board	69	Optometrist
Board	59	Energy Industry
Board Size: 9	Average Age: 63	

New York Community Bancorp, Inc.		
Position	Age	Profession
Chairman	84	Real Estate Developer/Retired
Lead Director	73	Accountant/Real Estate Developer
CEO	71	Banker
COO	63	Banker
Board	86	Insurance Agency
Board	62	Private Equity/Emerging Mkts
Board	75	Retired Banker
Board	73	Attorney/Retired
Board	65	Real Estate Developer
Board	79	Bank Regulator/Retired
Board	61	Accountant/Retired
Board	80	Retired Banker
Board Size: 12	Average Age: 73	

Hilltop Holdings Inc.		
Position	**Age**	**Profession**
Chairman	73	Private Investment/Retired Banker
Vice Chair-Co CEO	69	Banker
Co-CEO	43	Banker
Board	51	NFL Team Chief Brand Officer
Board	72	Securities/Retired
Board	53	Accountant and Consultant
Board	66	Oil & Gas Exploration/Retired
Board	64	Media and Telecom Investments
Board	81	Noise Abatement for Oil & Gas Industry
Board/Employee	71	Chairman of Hilltop Securities
Board	74	Private Investor/ Retired Investment Banker
Board	75	Attorney
Board	66	Construction
Board	57	Natural Gas
Board	80	Insurance Co./Retired
Board	69	Insurance Company

Board	52	Investment Advisor/Broker Dealer
Board	70	Retail Grocery
Board	68	Retired Banker
Board	73	Oilfield Services
Board Size: 20	Average Age: 66	

The average board size for this group was 12, and the average age was 66. The age was not noticeably different, but the board size was 20% higher than the Top 5 banks. I'm not sure this matters because Hilltop Holdings has a whopping 20 board members, skewing this number for the other four. Absent them, the Bottom 5 board size is similar to the Top 5.

So what is it about the Top 5 that differentiates it from the Bottom 5? In terms of bankers, active or retired, this group looks no different than the Top 5.

I will say there seems to be more PE, Investment Banker, Investment Management types on the Bottom 5 boards than on the Top 5. This might be explained by the capital formation process, where a low performing bank gets equity injections and those folks go on the board. Perhaps not. Either way, having Investment-type folks on your board doesn't seem to be the secret sauce to great shareholder returns.

So, as was my take from September 2016, there is no discernable difference between number of board members, age, professions of board members in top performing financial institutions and bottom dwellers.

Then, as now, my working theory is that the best boards are ones that approve strategy and hold management accountable for achieving it, and effectively dispatch their duties as described by the FDIC above. Each board member is an ingredient in the effectiveness of the entire board. And it doesn't matter if they are in Ag Supply or are the brand manager for the Dallas Cowboys.

What are your thoughts on an effective board?

~ Jeff

∞

Unfortunately, if you were reading this chapter hoping for clear-cut data that provide a magic bullet for an effective community bank board, you will be disappointed.

Still, though, the clues exist and are worth examining.

But before delving into ingredients for an effective board, let's go negative and review some of the attributes of an ineffective board. These are common traits, and are by no means exclusive to ineffective boards. A board may have one or many of these characteristics and still function as a productive body. But it would certainly be a body that is holding itself back.

Topping the list of attributes that make for an ineffective board is having members who are micromanagers. The tendency to micromanage plays out in countless ways. When I first published the research above, one reader, a banking industry consultant, left a telling example in the comment section. The consultant recalled a board member who voted against a bank-owned life insurance (BOLI) proposal because the vendor had one hand that appeared sun-kissed while the other hand was not. So the board member assumed the vendor spent a fair amount of time golfing, and therefore was apparently not suitable to advise the bank on BOLI. Clearly, there were several issues with that board member's decision-making process, but they all boil down to the board getting involved in management decisions.

Another attribute of an ineffective board is size—that is, it's either too big or too small. Do you think it's easy for the CEO of Hilltop Holdings, Inc. to communicate effectively with every member of a 20-person board? A board that's too large also runs the risk of developing factions, creating multiple centers of power, and rendering invisible otherwise skilled board members. Not only that, board succession becomes a major challenge.

Earlier in my career, my firm was helping a relatively new bank raise additional capital. This bank made the mistake of putting all significant investors on its board. The panel grew to 25 members—very difficult to manage. As I recall, only a few of them spoke up during board meetings. Most shrunk in their seats, allowing the most vocal to dominate. One board member regularly took personal calls while in meetings, cupping his hand over his mouth, assuming we couldn't hear him. Cell phones were clunky at the time. This board member erroneously thought he was invisible. The bank was sold before achieving any level of financial success.

Having too few board members can also be a challenge. Executing board responsibilities requires diverse skills, a distribution of responsibilities, and the climate for robust dialog among board members and between the board and management. Presiding over a small board may be easier on the chairman and CEO, but fewer hands make it more difficult to effectively execute on board responsibilities. Also, a small board runs a greater risk of being overly deferential to the CEO, which is characteristic of a bank that might perform well in the short-term but falls short of building a long-term, sustainable performance culture.

Case in point: Consider the five-person board that was overly deferential to a CEO who did not believe in technology. At the time of this writing (and you can check the copyright date), the bank had no debit cards, ATMs, online banking, or even a website. Would you challenge that strategy? Well this board didn't, and the bank runs the risk of its customers dying off. Literally.

So, what is the right-sized board? In a 2019 *Bank Director* magazine compensation study, the median board members for all surveyed banks was 10.[xii] To avoid tied votes, it's worth considering an odd number of directors, such as seven to 11. I have never witnessed a split vote in the boardroom before, so an odd-numbered board is not necessarily set in stone. If more than one employee sits on the board, consider the higher number. I would also think twice before putting more than two employees on the board, as this runs the risk of creating a built-in faction. Factions in board rooms frequently lead to dysfunction.

I have observed that the best functioning boards operate at the appropriate level, with a focus on strategy, compliance, and safety and soundness. These boards also embrace an institution's higher purpose, if they have one, and balance how they serve all stakeholders, not just shareholders. They are not dominated by one or two voices, and challenge each other and management.

And what of diversity? A very hot topic now, as it has been for years. But politics and popular opinion aside, what is the business case for a diverse board? Turns out, diversity in and of itself isn't necessarily correlated to better financial results or safer, sounder financial institutions. A University of Pennsylvania professor summed up the data on board gender diversity this way:

"Rigorous, peer-reviewed studies suggest that companies do not perform better when they have women on the board. Nor do they perform worse."[xxiii]

~ Katherine Klein, University of Pennsylvania

Professor Klein's opinion, given in 2017 and based on significant peer-reviewed research, is not consistent with today's conventional wisdom. But conventional wisdom, if it is to evolve to actual wisdom, should be based on observable facts.

I believe diversity is important to an effective community banking board. Although reasons for that are more complex than performance data, they are just as observable.

Groupthink is a critical challenge in bank board rooms. Walter Wrigley Jr. said, "When two men in a business always agree, one of them is unnecessary." Wrigley disliked yes-men. And so should you. Larry Fink, CEO of BlackRock, an investment management firm that is so large that it has investment positions in virtually all publicly traded financial institutions, said this:

"Boards with a diverse mix of genders, ethnicities, career experiences, and ways of thinking have, as a result, a more diverse and aware mindset. They are less likely to succumb to groupthink or miss new threats to a company's business model. And they

are better able to identify opportunities that promote long-term growth.[lxiv]

~ Larry Fink, CEO of BlackRock

The purpose for creating diversity on your board is not to make an altruistic gesture toward underrepresented populations. The main purpose is to bring diversity of thought to the boardroom, to benefit from the experiences of diverse professions, ages, geographies, and yes, races and genders. In case you haven't noticed, women and minorities are filling the professions that you should value as part of your professionally and geographically diverse board.

If your board includes your accountant, your lawyer, and two of your golfing buddies, how much will you challenge each other? Or worse, if the board includes the CEO's accountant, lawyer, and golfing buddies, how much will they challenge him or her?

Groupthink is an effective board's enemy. Many financial institutions mitigate this risk through their nominating and governance committee. These groups are typically responsible for whole-board and individual board member assessments, as well as nominating new directors—usually to fill vacant board seats left by retiring board members.

The nominating process merits attention. Too often, what I have witnessed is an informal recruiting process based on the personal relationships of existing board members. ("Hey Jeff, the board needs a CPA. Is your accountant interested?") If this is how it happens at your financial institution, is it any surprise that you're replenishing departing board members with acquaintances and people that look and think a lot like you? To strengthen your board, build discipline in your nominating process. Use board assessments to identify needed skills and geographies likely to help the board execute its duties. And find candidates from outside your circle of acquaintance.

Another challenge is when board members overstay their welcome. Once again, there's no panacea. One way to combat the challenge—which is not limited to financial institutions—is to institute a mandatory retirement age. This is a mistake. Would Warren Buffet be eligible for your board if you had a mandatory retirement age?

CalPERS, the agency that manages the California pension system, is one of the largest pension funds in the world. In its governance and sustainability principles, it suggests that board members can become overly familiar with each other, and therefore more likely to suffer groupthink, when they have been on the board for 12 years.[xv] Even, one presumes, if it is Warren Buffet. But for goodness sake, who would want to age Warren Buffet off their board? Rather than using the 12-year tenure as an automatic cutoff point, CalPERS uses it as a trigger for reevaluating the board member's independence.

To Sum It Up...

A board of directors is less the sum of its parts than it is a single organism. At a fundamental level, you want to construct your board to be the most effective organism possible at executing its roles and responsibilities. Toward that end, ask the right questions: Is it important to put the most talented IT professional on your board, even if he or she may not communicate effectively or interact well in a group? Or is it more important to put in a capable IT professional who helps the board evaluate your bank's IT budget and asks challenging and relevant questions of management? If the board needs a left arm, dispatch your nominating committee to find a left arm. The arm must work well with the right arm, the legs, the lungs, and the rest of the body. Because an arm alone is of no value.

Points Made This Chapter

❖ "What Makes an Effective Community Banking Board" drew the most interest of any banking topic I've covered.

❖ My research does not indicate an obvious correlation between financial performance/long-term shareholder returns and the professions, ages, or numbers of board members.

❖ When making decisions on board composition, always look first to board responsibilities as defined by your regulator and your company/bank.

❖ Think of your board as a single organism.

❖ Groupthink is a board's worst enemy.

❖ Age limits are a mistake. Consider CalPERS' 12-year rule to avoid familiarity. Also, use individual board member assessments to identify the keepers.

❖ Board size should be anywhere from seven to 11 members.

❖ Avoid putting more than two bank employees on your board to avoid factions. If you appoint two employees, set the number of board members at a higher limit (that is, 10 to 11).

❖ Develop and execute a disciplined nominating process that does not rely on board acquaintances.

❖ Board diversity matters primarily to avoid groupthink and improve strategic decisions that arrive at better outcomes.

Section II

No Amount of Good Execution Will Help a Bad Strategy

In a learning organization, allowing for failure and quickly

recognizing it is as critical as successful strategy execution.

Chapter 4

Bankers and Strategic Bets

The first ATM in the United States was deployed by Chemical Bank in New York City in 1969—two years after its initial appearance in Europe. It took another 15 years to reach widespread acceptance.[xvi] It was banking's great leap forward. Maybe more of a slow jog than a leap.

Mobile banking first deployed in earnest with the advent of the smart phone in 2007-08. It took four years for 21 percent of all smart phone owners to use mobile banking apps. From the Great Depression to the ATM, the slow pace of change in banking lulled us into complacency. We never had to rush toward shiny objects because we could wait and see whether they became mainstream without much penalty for patience. There was a greater penalty for early adoption, poor implementation, and sometimes failure. Why do it? Watch others wade into the deep end. Sip an umbrella drink and wait it out.

The development of the microprocessor in 1971 planted the seeds that would change the world forever. But most of us had no way to know it at the time. The great technology acceleration in banking didn't gather steam until the 1990s, after a sluggish technology adoption that started far sooner. What began as the tortoise is evolving to the hare. Are bankers still developing and executing strategy at tortoise pace?

This was the context that led to the article below. Here's what I wrote.

∞

Bankers and Strategic Bets. A Slow Embrace

March 3, 2018

https://www.jeff4banks.com/2018/03/bankers-and-strategic-bets-slow-embrace.html

There are a lot of crazy ideas out there in banking causing us to think... "remember when such and such ridiculous idea was the new craze?" And we would laugh, continue to drink our cocktail, and lament that another financial institution threw in the towel to merge with a bigger brother.

That's what I thought about while reading a recent Financial Brand post about Innovation in Banking: Killer Ideas? or Idea Killers?[xvii] More talk about fintech, dinosaur bankers, and flavors of the month.

But their animation caught my attention. And it stirred images of a few strategic planning sessions I have moderated. Much to my chagrin.

How do we balance strategic direction, customer demand, and the futurist or wildly over-caffeinated millennial that tells us we have to implement every shiny new object or we'll die?

Six years ago I asked in a blog post Will Plain Vanilla Kill Community Banking?[xviii] Did I get caught up in the change-or-die crowd? Was I, gulp, a futurist? When I wrote that post in January 2011 there were

7,700 FDIC insured financial institutions. Today there are less than 5,700. A 26% decline. Was I a futurist?

This brings me to the subject of Strategic Bets. They can be a strategic shift of your franchise, a new product line, or a new operating environment. Something you are not doing, will require some investment to do, and risks failing miserably. Bankers are slow to embrace strategic bets, opting for tweaks to business as usual. Which runs the risk of making the cartoon above become a reality.

Let me highlight some strategic bets for you. In the above blog post, I discussed Apple and Bank of New York Mellon.

Sticking with the Apple theme, in 2007, they launched the iPhone. Here was a personal computer company that decided... "mobile phones, yeah, mobile phones". Much like they did "digital music, yeah, digital music. Thanks Napster!" in the early 2000's.

How about Amazon? When they started in 1995, they sold books. Maybe those millennial futurists don't remember this. Online book stores. Competing with Barnes and Noble and Borders? In 1998, they decided "why don't we sell everything online?" And boom! Now my friend orders toilet paper through Amazon Prime.

Apple, Inc.	Sales (000)		Sales (000)	
	2015	%	2017	%
iPhone	$155,041	66.3%	$141,319	61.6%
iPad	23,227	9.9%	19,222	8.4%
Mac	25,471	10.9%	25,850	11.3%
Services (ApplePay, iTunes, etc.)	19,909	8.5%	29,980	13.1%
Other Products (TV, Watch, Beats)	10,067	4.3%	12,863	5.6%
Total Sales	$233,715	100.0%	$229,234	100.0%
Amazon.com Inc.				
Online Stores	$76,863	71.8%	$108,354	60.9%
Physical Stores	0	0.0%	5,798	3.3%
Third Party Sellers (commissions, fulfillment, etc.)	16,086	15.0%	31,881	17.9%
Subscription Services (Prime, etc.)	4,467	4.2%	9,721	5.5%
AWS (Web services)	7,880	7.4%	17,459	9.8%
Other (selling services, co-branded credit cards)	1,710	1.6%	4,653	2.6%
Total Sales	$107,006	100.0%	$177,866	100.0%

*Source: SEC.gov Apple's fiscal period ends Sep. 30th.

The iPhone represents 62% of Apple sales. Didn't even exist in 2006. Physical stores grew from nothing to 3.3% of Amazon sales and is likely to grow. Because Amazon, with their culture of online sales and fulfillment, had that strategic bet meeting where they agreed "new-fangled brick and mortar store, yeah, let's do that."

Some other strategic bets that have the chance to transform or have transformed a company:

Pepsi - I listened to a podcast where Indra Nooyi, their CEO said they are focusing on their "healthy for you" line. Pepsi? Also, they are developing female friendly snacks. Apparently females like snacks that don't crunch loudly or leave a residue on your fingers, and fit into a purse.

Overstock - Announced this year they are getting into Robo Advising. They have a heavily female customer base, and see opportunity to build an offering attractive to those that visit their stores and online space.

Leader Bank - A $1.2 billion in assets Massachusetts bank

developed Zrent so it's landlord customers could more efficiently collect rent from tenants. The bank now licenses the product to other financial institutions.

SunTrust - Developed Lightstream, a national online lending platform to provide consumer loans for practically any purpose. Its proprietary technology gives consumers a virtually paperless experience.

I think there are enough examples of strategic bets transforming businesses. Combined with the alarming rate of those that don't take strategic bets deciding to sell, shouldn't you be thinking about calculated strategic bets that could become a significant part of your future success?

~ Jeff

∞

Technology doesn't drive the bank. People do. And people use technology to efficiently and effectively process transactions, monitor compliance, balance the books, and inform customers and employees. It is not a bank product or service. It is a tool. Like the abacus or calculator. So strategic bets are not about using this tool over that tool. Strategic bets are about allocating resources to initiatives that will make you relevant, maybe even important, to the future of your stakeholders. If your strategy was to build a village in the woods, for example, would a chain saw or hand saw be more efficient? Don't get strategic bets mixed up with the tools to execute on them.

If your culture is to manage by budget instead of budget by strategy, how likely are you to implement a strategic bet? Because strategic bets generally take longer than the next fiscal year to yield results. That wasn't always the case when our industry was closer to the tortoise than the hare. Acquiring a lender or team of lenders might be expensive, at least initially. But the payoff happens when their book of business migrates to our bank. Usually that's well within the first year of joining the new institution.

Today the payoff might require a much longer timeline. Are we willing to accept that? History indicates that we are. Branching is exhibit one. During the prolific branching of the 1990s and the 2000s—leading up to the 2008 financial crisis—we popped branches like chicklets into every town and hamlet across the country. And many, if not most, of those branches failed to reach desired profitability within three years. Heck, some haven't hit their mark in over a decade. But we built them, staffed them, and continue to support them. So taking a flyer on a long-term strategy is not new to banking.

I'm not convinced that "to branch or not to branch" is the strategic bet. Look one level higher. "*Can* we make a difference in this community?" is the bet, in my opinion. And if your analysis says "yes we can," the branching question is next level—as in, "*how* do we make a difference in this community?" A branch could be the means to a more noble and strategic end. If your branch fails to achieve desired profitability within a reasonable period of time, then the failure of the strategic bet could be in its execution, or in the bet itself. One can be fixed by executing on the bet differently. The other means we were mistaken that there was a legitimate opportunity to make a difference in that particular community. We made a wrong bet.

Consider exhibit two: a Southwestern community bank that

determined it could reduce in-branch transaction demands—and thereby reduce branch staff—by implementing interactive teller machines (ITMs). To what end? Was this part of a higher-level strategy to allow branch employees to focus on loans, advice, and problem solving? Or was it to cut costs and improve profits?

Neither of these goals was achieved. Although staffing levels in the branches declined, costs did not. Expenses simply migrated to hardware and software, i.e., the ITMs, plus increased staffing in the call center. There were no net savings. And since there were no savings, the strategic bet did not free up resources to invest in the development of branch staff to excel at lending, giving advice, or problem solving. If the strategic bet was to employ ITMs to reduce branch transactions, it was a win. If it was to redirect resources from staffing levels to enhanced branch capabilities or to the bank's bottom line, this strategic bet failed.

Afraid of Failure?

"Failure is success in progress."
~ Albert Einstein

Einstein's words couldn't be further from the truth in banking. *"Nothing ventured, nothing to arouse regulator scrutiny"* is closer to my experience. Failure avoidance culture is pervasive in this industry. Is it a result of the slow pace of change from the Great Depression until the 1990s? Or is it the fact that banking is highly regulated, and experimentation—coupled with the necessary failure or two—surely draws enhanced regulatory attention? Or the fact that regulatory attention subjects bank management to regulator whimsy under the guise of safety and soundness? Or…perhaps we have found the enemy, and it is us.

Banks commit a monumental amount of energy to being 100 percent in compliance, minimizing mistakes, and avoiding any possible audit findings or (gasp) "Matters Requiring Attention" on their exams. Some operations managers' evaluations—and, in some circumstances, variable compensation—is dependent on clean audits. What does that get you? Hyper-conservatism in experimentation in the name of compliance. And a whole lot of "we can't do it" from executives. We have gotten away with it for so long because the race has been run by other tortoises. But that can't last.

To accelerate our evolution and improve our relevance to younger customers, we should allow experimentation. Make strategic bets. And (gasp) accept failure. I'm not talking "bet the bank" failure. But a failure that may bust your budget is not Armageddon. It is an opportunity to learn, adjust, and better implement the next innovation. It is never a reason to avoid strategic bets for 10 years and think, "We tried and failed 10 years ago and, dag nabbit, we are not goin' to try again!"

The Strategy of the Strategic Bet

Strategy forces banks to look far out into the future. Running by budget, on the other hand, forces bankers to look no further than next year. It's the difference between being ready for where the puck is going, versus positioning yourself where it is. We intuitively know, I believe, that our industry would not have yielded so much market share to branchless banks and nonbank service providers if we could think outside of our budgets.

If consumers' banking habits changed at the same pace as their technology consumption, we would already be out of business. Look at how Apple has survived. Sometime in the mid to late 1990s, a clairvoyant leader at Apple thought that Mac sales would not drive this company forward. So they strategized. They determined where computing was going. They widened their strategic thinking to the world of multi-media and telecommunications. Where could they make a difference, be a first mover, corner a market? And they transformed their company to something materially different from what it once was.

If you think community financial institutions don't have the capacity for that type of strategic betting, look no further than River Valley Bank in Wisconsin. The bank was a family owned, primarily agricultural bank in the mid-1980s. Seeing the limitations in its own existing markets—and its digital capabilities—the bank responded by opening an online division in 2009 called IncredibleBank. At that time, the bank had $950 million in total assets, net income of $8.7 million, and an ROA of 0.94 percent. Not bad for a bank at the tail of the financial crisis. So why make a strategic bet?

Bank executives saw the challenges in their markets. They saw the changes in customer preferences. They saw large banks investing in technology. They predicted where the puck was going. Ten years after making the IncredibleBank strategic bet, the bank had grown to $1.4 billion, had net income of $21.6 million, and an ROA of 1.58 percent. The bet was so successful, they rebranded their entire bank as IncredibleBank.

What if the bet had failed? After assessing whether the failure was due to execution or incorrectly predicting where the puck was going, the bank could have shut down its online division and continued forward as

River Valley Bank. Or it could have shifted strategy away from promoting an affinity brand and into an additional funding source. Would the failed bet have cost money? Yes. Would it have directed resources away from a potentially more promising one? Yes. But would the bank be where it is today if it had not made the bet? The answer is clear.

Sutton Bank in Attica, Ohio is another case in point. An ostensibly traditional community bank, it does commercial real estate, commercial business, ag, and residential real estate lending. What's not so traditional: 53 percent of its deposits are non-interest bearing, its ROA has been recorded over 3 percent, and its ROE 30 percent. Why the eye-popping numbers?

At some point in the late 1990s and early 2000s, Sutton sponsored digital banks: Depaulbank.com and Aueaglebank.com. It was also one of the earliest banks in prepaid cards, with the eCelerate program for the multi-level direct sales company, Amway. Since that time, Sutton has issued hundreds of card programs, building strong partnerships with card networks, processors, and program managers. From these origins the bank has transitioned from an issuing organization to a payments facilitator.

In 2010, the bank had combined revenue (net interest income plus fee income) of $15.7 million, with 28 percent of that revenue from fees. That's much higher than the 10-20 percent of revenue that traditional community banks typically derive from fees. And in 2019, the bank had $37.1 million in total revenue, with 46 percent from fees—mostly prepaid card revenue. Sutton Bank's strategic bet was on payments, and it paid off handsomely. Imagine where they'd be now if their strategy team at a planning retreat years ago had settled for whatever they did the previous year, plus 5 percent.

To Sum It Up...

Change is accelerating in the banking industry. That alone should give pause to strategists who would consider walking out of a strategic planning meeting with only slight modifications to "business as usual." Perhaps you think your target customers—the ones who generate a disproportionate share of profits—are stuck in the mud and resistant to the change happening around them. For many years, banks have gotten a pass because many of those customers have indeed been slower to change. But do you really know who those customers are now and how their needs are changing? The clock is ticking. Slight modifications to business as usual might just be riskier than making the strategic bets that will lead your institution forward. So make them. Research, test, implement, fail, learn, make course corrections, test and implement again, succeed.

Points made this chapter:

❖ It took the ATM 15 years to gain widespread acceptance. It took mobile banking four. The cycle of technology adoption to acceptance is faster today and will be even faster tomorrow.

❖ Fintech prognosticators always predict the demise of banks if they don't do this or that. In terms of direction, they are generally correct. In terms of timing, they are nearly always wrong.

❖ A strategic bet is a strategic shift of your franchise, a new product line, or a new operating environment. In other words, it involves something you are not already doing, that will require some investment to accomplish, and that carries the risk of failing miserably.

❖ People drive the bank. Technology is a tool.

❖ To accelerate our evolution and improve our relevance to our target customers, it's necessary to allow experimentation. To make strategic bets. And (gasp) to occasionally fail.

❖ Research is essential determine where the puck is going. Strategy forces banks to look far out into the future. Running by budget, on the other hand, forces bankers to focus on next year.

❖ There are plenty of examples of strategic bets transforming a company for the better. Look to Amazon, Apple, IncredibleBank, and Sutton Bank. There are plenty more. Put your institution on the list.

Chapter 5

Is There Such a Thing as Too Much Capital?

How effectively do you deploy your capital? This question is particularly important in capital intensive businesses like banking. Whether or not you are shareholder owned, the question still applies. The stakeholders may be partially different. But your board will judge the bank's success by how well you deploy other peoples' money, i.e., your capital.

Banking sometimes plays out like a Hatfield and McCoy feud when it comes to effective capital deployment. Some stakeholders, recounting the various recessionary periods throughout their careers, believe capital is king and there is no such thing as too much of it. Their financial metric of choice is return on assets (ROA), because there is little downside to holding too much capital, and not enough upside of leveraging it to the hilt.

Others—those who classify themselves as more shareholder friendly—prefer return on equity (ROE) as the go-to metric for financial performance. The ROE aficionados are more inclined to leverage the balance sheet to the point of skirting with their capital plan's target capital ratios, or regulatory "well-capitalized" status. Having a significant capital buffer while entering a recessionary period may help the ROA gang sleep at night, but the excess capital makes the ROE gang uncomfortable during economic expansions.

Who is right? The question is most assuredly on bankers' minds. I have written a number of articles on the topic, and three of them were in the top 20 most read. I cover them in this chapter in a logical sequence.

Here are my thoughts over the recent years on the subject of too much capital, along with ideas for deploying it.

∞

For Financial Institutions, Is There Such A Thing As Too Much Capital? Yes. Yes There Is.

July 28, 2018

https://www.jeff4banks.com/2018/07/for-financial-institutions-is-there.html

I was on a panel at a bankers conference with an investment banker and two bank fund investors. One of the investors' opening remarks was about banks that were over-capitalized. I panned the audience to see if regulators were present.

But there were enough open jaw gapes to see that many bankers share the regulatory belief that there is no such thing as too much capital. And that may be true for financial institutions that don't take investor money. But if your bank is shareholder owned, then you may be hoarding their money. And as a bank shareholder myself, I like to make my own hoarding decisions.

I have written on these pages about a method to estimate your "well capitalized",[xix] a question your regulators may have asked you. Having done this, and seeing that your strategic plan has you comfortably above your well capitalized and trending higher, what do you do with the excess capital?

Derek McGee of Austin law firm Fenimore, Kay, Harrison, and Ford had four to-the-point ideas in a recent Bank Director Magazine article.[xx] I would like to lay out his four ideas with my take on them.

1. Dividends. "Returning excess capital to shareholders through enhanced dividend payouts increases the current income stream provided to shareholders and is often a well-received option. However, in evaluating the appropriate level of dividends, including whether to commence paying or increase dividends, banks should be aware of two potential issues. First, an increase in dividends is often difficult to reverse, as shareholders generally begin to plan for the income stream associated with the enhanced dividend payout. Second, the payment of dividends does not provide liquidity to those shareholders looking for an exit. Accordingly, dividends, while representing an efficient option for deploying excess capital, presents other considerations that should be evaluated in the context of a bank's strategic planning."

My take: Amen Derek! In a recent article I wrote, Bank Dividends: Go Ahead and Drink the Kool Aid[xxi], I called for the same thing. And to use special dividends and deliberate shareholder communications to help overcome shareholder expectations mentioned above. I have not experienced a bank that made the pivot from being a growth company to a cash cow, where profits are maximized and dividends are plentiful. It is a natural evolution of a company built to endure.

2. Stock Repurchases. "Stock repurchases, whether through a tender offer, stock repurchase plan or other discretionary stock repurchase, enhance liquidity of investment for selling shareholders, while creating value for non-selling shareholders by increasing their stake in the bank. Following a stock repurchase, bank earnings are spread over a smaller shareholder base, which increases earnings per share and the value of each share. Stock purchases can be a highly effective use of excess capital, particularly where the bank believes its stock is undervalued. Because repurchases can be conducted through a number of vehicles, a bank may balance its desire to effectively deploy a targeted amount of excess capital against its need to maintain operational flexibility."

My take: Institutional shareholders own greater than two thirds of publicly traded financial institutions' shares outstanding. And share buybacks are a favorite of theirs. The challenge is that they would like to liquidate their ownership when the value is at its peak. Meaning the financial institution purchasing its shares would likely enjoy minimal earnings accretion and create book value dilution. But, as Derek pointed out, it is a highly effective use of excess capital when the bank believes it is undervalued. One bank stock analyst thinks every bank should calculate the earnings accretion of a prospective merger versus the earnings accretion of a share buyback. If the buyback is more accretive, why do a riskier merger?

3. De Novo Expansion in Vibrant Markets. "Banks can also reinvest excess capital through organic expansion into new markets through de novo branching and the acquisition of key deposit or loan officers."

My take: When a race car enters the pits, it is losing time. If not to recalibrate, refuel, and re-tire, drivers wouldn't do it. If you compare bank strategy to a 500-mile race, banks would also enter the pits. But if you compare bank strategy to a few times around the track, you would be foolish to do so. Think of the short race as budgets, and the 500-miler as strategy. You have to be willing to accept the short-term setback of entering the pits (i.e. making strategic investments like Derek mentioned) to position you to win the race.

4. Mergers & Acquisitions. "Banks can deploy excess capital to jumpstart growth through merger and acquisition opportunities. In general, size and scale boost profitability metrics and enhance earnings growth, and mergers and acquisitions can be an efficient mechanism to generate size and scale. Any successful acquisition must be complementary from a strategic standpoint, as well as from a culture perspective."

My take: Derek's "complementary" comment was right on. Listen to my firm's most recent podcast on M&A cultural integration featuring an interview with Jim Vaccaro, Chairman and CEO of Manasquan Bank, that is in the process of merger integration as I type.[xxii] In addition to a cultural fit, the geography and balance sheets should be complementary, and the earnings accretion should exceed what the buying institution could achieve on its own. Tangible book value dilution, which tends to get a lot of play in the investment media, should not be to the level to cause long-term downward pressure on the buyer's stock price.

Out of the four, M&A is the least within the control of the financial institution, as this takes a willing partner.

What other uses of excess capital do you propose?

~ Jeff

∞

The natural evolution of a company—any company—is to grow at a pace the company can sustain and the markets permit. Ideally, growth should continue until you achieve the necessary economies of scale for cost efficiency, but have not yet grown too large to deliver on your vision and mission. The risk of too much growth is you may run into diseconomies of scale, or the law of large numbers, in which it takes incredible effort to replace amortizing and maturing loans. At this inflection point, banks tend to move off of their vision and mission and start to chase larger and larger, more commoditized deals.

Once a bank reaches this point, I advise management teams and boards to review their dividend policies. And the solution often varies for different management teams operating with different business models in different markets.

Case in point: The First National Bank of Alaska pays regular cash dividends that are 70 percent of earnings. In 2019, the bank declared a special dividend that upped the payout ratio to 82 percent. Why so high, when most financial institutions typically pay out far less than 50 percent of earnings? The bank's leverage ratio was 13.8 percent at the end of 2019. And although its ROA was an impressive 1.47 percent, its ROE was a pedestrian 10.47 percent. The bank's asset quality was solid. But it had too much capital. And poof! Special dividend. Why hoard shareholder money?

I have heard the double taxation argument, which points out that the corporation pays taxes on income, and then shareholders pay on the dividend. But isn't it the same situation with buybacks? The corporation buys back its shares using cash that is there because of its net income—and shareholders are then taxed on capital gains. In both situations, individual taxes are deferred if the stock resides in a retirement vehicle, like a traditional IRA.

One approach that was not previously mentioned in my article or the Derek McGee piece is a depositor-directed "special dividend." This method of deploying excess capital may be less enticing to shareholder-owned institutions than mutual banks or credit unions. For a bank that balances how it serves its stakeholders, it can be an attractive option. Bear in mind, the concept of the special dividend is separate and distinct from the consistently attractive rates offered by some mutuals. The CEO of one New Jersey mutual, for example, feels it is his obligation to return capital to depositors in the form of attractive rates. Depositors to this institution can rely on their bank to always pay top-of-market rate on deposits.

But I'm not convinced this is the best way to deploy excess capital. That's because "best rate" banks attract rate-sensitive customers. They are only loyal if you keep delivering the rate. And that business model requires a hyper-inexpensive infrastructure because it's a low-margin business. Unless you have high yielding assets on the other side, like Capital One with its credit cards. Without higher yielding assets, you'll be counting paper clips like Ace Greenberg of Bear Stearns.

The special depositor dividend is a different story. First, it's a pre-tax event, so Uncle Sam pays for a chunk of it. Second, you can select who gets it. Think of your core depositors (checking, savings, money market) who have some loyalty to your bank (such as customers for over one year). Third, because it is "special," if your institution is having a bad year or your markets are in recession, you don't have to pay it. With the special dividend you are deploying excess capital to an important constituency to the success of your institution. What a great word-of-mouth marketing tool.

How Much Is Too Much?

"Too much" is a relative term. How much is too much? The answer, as it relates to capital, is not simple. It depends on the risk on your balance sheet, your projected growth, the resilience of your markets, and the economic cycle. Through Basel III, regulators—both U.S. domestic and international—have provided specific definitions of what is considered "well-capitalized." And most bankers defer to these when determining whether they have too little, too much, or just enough capital.

Are these measures correct for your institution? You might think it doesn't matter because your bank will be measured against them by your regulators, a key, next-level constituency. But I have heard countless times that regulators ask bankers: "What is *your* well-capitalized?" Bankers view this question as a trick to get them to identify some number above the regulatory definition—and fear they'll be held to account for the higher hurdle in their next exam. That assessment might be correct. During an exam exit interview, regulators once asked a bank CEO why the bank's total risk-based capital ratio was 20 basis points off its strategic plan projections. Twenty basis points! For a strategic planner, getting that close should be considered a win.

Whether it's a trick or not, banks should calculate their definition of "just enough" capital based on the risks on their balance sheet, their anticipated growth, and their risk appetite. But how?

This was the topic of another highly read article. Do you think the topic is important to bankers and other industry professionals? Why would they visit these articles over and over, downloading the tables, and asking follow-up questions? It is reassuring to know that they're keenly interested in how well they deploy and nurture capital.

Here is what I wrote on calculating how much capital is just enough.

∞

Risk Adjusted Return on Capital (RAROC) for Financial Institutions

May 28, 2012

https://www.jeff4banks.com/2012/05/risk-adjusted-return-on-capital-raroc.html

How do you measure the profitability of lines of business, products, or customers? The simplest form is in dollars. But does that measure the profits against the investment required to generate those profits? For example, the riskiest banking products most likely deliver the greatest dollar profits, all other things being equal. At least until the risk comes to roost.

Another means to measure profits is the ratio of profits to the size of the portfolio being measured. In banking, we call it the Return on Assets (ROA). For example, a $500 million commercial loan portfolio will have a greater dollar profit than a $100 million consumer loan portfolio, all things being equal. But the ROA of the consumer loan portfolio could be greater. But ROA does not measure the risk of what is being measured, just the relative profit contribution regardless of size.

Banking is a risk business, and has many internal and external factors that impact the amount of risk per activity. This is one reason that financial institutions are getting serious about viewing risk across the entire franchise instead of in the organizational silos where they most exist. See my post on Enterprise Wide Risk Management on this subject.[xxiii]

But through it all, risk requires capital. Look at the capital needed through the recent recessionary period for credit losses provided by either private investors or the US Treasury. Regulators assign risk weightings as a proxy for how much capital is needed based on the perceived risk of the asset. For example, a security in the investment portfolio may be 20% risk weighted, versus a loan that is 100% risk weighted. The total risk based capital ratio required by regulators to maintain "well capitalized" status formally remains 10%. So $100 million of 20% risk-weighted bonds requires $2 million of capital ($100 x 20% x 10%) versus $100 million of 100% risk-weighted loans requiring $10 million of capital.

If the amount of capital needed for a line of business, a product, or a customer varies based on risk, then it makes sense to measure the profitability of what is measured based on capital required. In industry parlance, we call that Risk Adjusted Return on Capital, or RAROC.

Financial institutions should assess on their own the amount of capital needed per product based on past experience, perceived risk, and potential loss. The table below shows how capital is allocated to each loan category based on a limited risk spectrum (credit, interest rate, and liquidity). Although for loans, these are probably the greatest risks, the financial institution may quantify other risks, such as operational (could it lose money due to fraud, hacking, etc.) or pricing (does the value of the asset fluctuate in the market, causing volatility and therefore risk).

Schmidlap National Bank
RAROC Analysis

	Low		Medium		High
Risk Rating Scale	1	2	3	4	5
Capital Assignment	0%	3%	6%	9%	12%

		Credit	Interest Rate	Liquidity	Composite	Assigned Capital	Capital ($000)
Risk Categories							
Risk Weights		55%	35%	10%	100%		
	Balance ($000)						
Loans:							
Commercial & Industrial	200,000	4	2	2	3.10	6.30%	12,600
Commercial Real Estate	400,000	2	4	4	2.90	5.70%	22,800
Construction	60,000	5	2	2	3.65	7.95%	4,770
Consumer	50,000	3	3	3	3.00	6.00%	3,000
Residential Real Estate	150,000	2	4	4	2.90	5.70%	8,550
Total Loans	860,000					6.01%	51,720

I perform such an analysis for an ABA School of Bank Marketing Management course that I teach every May. For my efforts I have been criticized that the topic was too complicated and I should remove it. But the course is on product profitability. How should I measure the relative profitability of business checking versus a home equity loan? Risk and the capital to support that risk should be the denominator in that equation. Agree? I say the topic stays. I'll take my lumps in the course evaluations.

What does your FI use as the profitability denominator?

~ Jeff

∞

In looking at the table from the article, the reader could make a quick calculation that the $860 million loan portfolio would be a $785 million risk-weighted portfolio if residential mortgages were weighted at 50 percent risk and all other loans at 100 percent. Under U.S. prompt corrective action capital rules, the bank would have to carry $78.5 million of capital—10 percent of risk-weight, or 9.13 percent of the total portfolio—to be considered well-capitalized. The 6 percent in the table, or $52 million, would not be enough.

Regulators only require capital to be allocated to assets. We know from our Asset-Liability Committee meetings that our liabilities have risk too. Sure, there is minimal credit risk, but not zero. Why else would we perform credit write-ups for remote deposit capture (RDC) or ACH customers? And there is plenty of interest rate risk and liquidity risk, not to mention operational risk, with our deposits. Risk requires capital. Don't box yourself in by estimating the capital you need based on assets alone. They should inform what you consider well-capitalized, but not drive it.

The Basel III model is a good example of using buffers to determine well-capitalized. And I encourage readers to determine if this method is right for your capital plan. A buffer method works like this: regulators deem a 5 percent leverage ratio to be well capitalized. You can set that as your minimum capital against each asset category and add a risk buffer to each, based on the various risk categories that impact that asset. So your loan portfolio might require 8 percent capital, including a 5 percent minimum plus a 3 percent risk buffer. Very similar to the Basel III method. On the liability side, no need for the 5 percent minimum. But continue to add the buffer based on the risk of the liability. And voila! You have *your* well-capitalized.

This method could go straight down to the individual loan, investment security, and deposit level. In fact, another article that landed in the top 20 most read was on loan pricing. The table in the article received significant attention and downloads.

Here is what I wrote.

∞

Loan Pricing: Must It Be So Complicated?

September 6, 2013

https://www.jeff4banks.com/2013/09/loan-pricing-must-it-be-so-complicated.html

When it comes to pricing loans, my experience tells me we use competitor pricing as our de facto pricing model. For consumer and residential loans, where rates and fees appear on the competitors' websites, it's not so difficult. But for commercial loans, I suspect we follow anecdotes such as what customers tell us or what friendly competitors murmur to us at a cocktail party. We tell loan committees that this is the rate and structure needed to "get the deal done".

In comes the loan pricing models. Some are expensive. Some are free, such as the one recently mentioned by my friend Dallas Wells of Asset Management Group, an ALCO consulting firm based in Kansas City.

Now, I have never been a commercial lender. But I'm a student of the lending function, and listen intently to senior managers discuss loan pricing in profitability improvement meetings that I moderate. That's where I hear the stories of the competition, irrational pricing, yadda yadda yadda.

I recently had two students from the Pacific Coast Bankers School (PCBS) ask me about how to risk price loans. Why they asked me, I don't know. Although I'm no loan pricing expert, I have my opinions. And my opinion is it should not be as complicated as those "in the know" would like us to believe. So for you, fair readers, I developed this simple loan pricing model (see table).

Jeff-For-Banks
Easy to Use, Easy to Understand, Loan Pricing Tool

1	Hurdle Pre-Tax ROE	20.00%
	Inputs	
2	Loan Amount	$1,000,000
3	Loan Type[1]	583
4	Internal Credit Rating	5
5	Loan Duration (years)[2]	4.3
	Auto Inputs and Calculations	
6	Transfer Price (Cost of Funds)[3]	2.12%
7	Capital Allocation[4]	8.04%
8	Operating Cost Per Account[5]	$3,023
9	Operating Cost Per Account (%)	0.30%
10	Provision Expense (%)[6]	0.35%
11	Required Pre-Tax Profit	$16,080
12	Recommended Minimum Loan Yield	4.38%

1 Type Code that drives capital allocation from RAROC model
2 Derived by Loan Repricing, Duration, and/or Cash Flows
3 Provided by Finance based on Loan Repricing, Duration and/or Cash Flows
4 Capital Allocation determined by RAROC analysis
   based on Type Code and Internal Credit Rating
5 Determined by Product Profitability or Industry Benchmarks
6 Determined by ALLL methodology

Four inputs, you say? Well, there is some back room gears at work too. For example, the loan duration should be calculated by the loan cash flows and repricing characteristics. Is it a five year, 20 year amortizing commercial real estate loan? Then perhaps the cash flow calculation pegs the loan duration at 4.3 years, as it does in this model.

The transfer price, or charging the lender a cost of funds for the borrowed money, is typically derived from a rate index, such as the Federal Home Loan Bank yield curve, for the same duration borrowing.

That would have to come from Finance and be blended for odd-lot terms, such as 4.3 years.

Capital allocation should be determined by a risk adjusted return on capital model (RAROC). I described this in greater detail in a previous post. But this analysis would have previously occurred, and be assigned based on loan type code and the internal risk rating.

If your bank performs product profitability, a natural calculation from this model is operating cost per account based on type code. If you do not have product profitability, you can analyze your approximate operating cost per account or use industry benchmarks.

And lastly, the provision expense associated with this type of loan and risk rating should be driven by your Allowance for Loan and Lease Loss (ALLL) methodology. You already do this, I guarantee it (insert Men's Warehouse founder voice).

There you have it. Now you have a well-priced loan that accounts for credit risk through the provision and RAROC calculations. Interest Rate Risk is accounted for in the transfer price, as this is taken from the same duration market instrument. You also account for other key risks through RAROC such as liquidity and compliance risk.

Price by this method, and you are accounting for the risks, costs, and desired margin of each loan. You can overlay deposit products to hit your ROE targets in a similar vein.

Price by this method, and you can determine if doing a loan at a certain price point, as told to you by your borrower, may or may not be a mutually beneficial pricing structure. Banking is one industry where success is driven not only by your ability to build relationships that are not price driven, but also by not being as stupid as your competitors. If the market price is too low for your appetite, have the courage to walk away.

What else should be considered in pricing a loan?

~ Jeff

∞

Circling back to capitalization, note that row 7 and note 4 of the loan pricing table tell a lot in a little space. If the hypothetical loan type code 583 is the five year, 20-year amortization commercial real estate loan with an internal credit rating of 5, then that requires an 8.04 percent capital allocation. Imagine having these calculations in your product risk assessments, refined by actual product performance during full economic cycles. Most commercial loan pricing models assign capital so bankers can calculate pre-tax ROE and set pricing hurdle rates. Unfortunately, many financial institutions use their software's default capital allocation rather than assigning capital at the instrument level, based on their own assessments and back testing.

By using this method, *your* well-capitalized could be calculated from the bottom up. Imagine the cultural evolution if each lender, branch manager, and cash management specialist were held accountable for their portfolio's pre-tax, risk adjusted return on capital instead of production or balance growth. Would that branch manager desperately call the head of retail for a certificate of deposit rate exception for a large depositor to keep the money in the bank? Or would you empower the branch manager to make those decisions (within certain guidelines of course)? If RAROC was their yardstick, culture and strategic alignment could be achieved. And the question of too much, too little, or just enough capital would be answered.

To Sum It Up...

The question of how much capital is enough is a relative question. It depends on the risk associated with the bank's balance sheet, projected growth, markets, and the economic cycle. This chapter covers a lot of ground because bankers continually demonstrate a strong interest in capital deployment, RAROC, and capital assignment. Whether a bank is owned by its shareholders or its depositors, its ability to effectively build and deploy its capital reflects how effectively the board and executive team manage the bank.

Points Made This Chapter

❖ Your board will judge your bank's success by how well it deploys other peoples' money, i.e., the bank's capital.

❖ If capital is king, and deploying it well is the measurement of success, there *is* such a thing as too much capital.

❖ There are multiple options for deploying excess capital. The best choice depends on the wants and needs of the financial institution's stakeholders.

❖ Regulators require capital to be allocated to assets but not to liabilities. But we know from experience that risk resides on both sides of the balance sheet.

❖ Bankers can measure their own well-capitalized by assessing the risk of all asset and liability categories on their balance sheet using the risk assessment process and back testing through various economic cycles.

❖ Assigning capital at the instrument level and maintaining RAROC accountabilities throughout the institution can serve to create cultural and strategic alignment.

Chapter 6

Does Your Institution Achieve Positive

Operating Leverage?

Your next $100 in revenue should cost less than the previous $100. The efficiency ratio (non-interest expense/(net interest income plus fee income)) and expense ratio (non-interest expense/average assets) should be less for the next $100 million in asset growth versus your prior $100 million. Are they?

This is the fundamental question of this chapter. And it's easy to calculate. Not as easy to achieve. Achieving and maintaining positive operating leverage requires discipline.

Operating leverage should not be confused with financial leverage. With the latter, an organization borrows money to increase revenue faster than debt service alone. That's how financial institutions typically consider leveraging the balance sheet to deploy capital to maximize revenue.

Operating leverage, on the other hand, is a culture. It's the discipline that ensures that expense and efficiency ratios come down when the bank achieves the full economic benefit of an investment such as a merger, a new technology, or a geographic or line-of-business expansion. It's what ultimately raises ROA, risk adjusted return on capital, and ROE, all other things being equal.

As such, operating leverage is a big-picture concept. If you're implementing 10 initiatives, and seven achieve the projected economic benefit while three do not, positive operating leverage should still be the result. If you strive for organizational learning and the ability to adapt to an environment that changes faster than ever—and where investments are riskier—you have to allow for failure and mitigate its impact.

The analysis in the below article, nearly a decade old, still rings true today, as evidenced by the many readers who continue to seek it out. Consider how using a similar analysis as an accountability tool would benefit your bank moving forward.

∞

Does Your Bank Achieve Positive Operating Leverage?

May 1, 2011

https://www.jeff4banks.com/2011/05/does-your-bank-achieve-positive.html

When a significant portion of your cost structure is fixed, then growing revenues should generate positive operating leverage... the cost of generating the next $100 of revenue should be less expensive than generating the previous $100. This fundamental logic stands behind the banking industry buzzphrase, economies of scale. The fixed cost of your IT infrastructure is less on a relative basis for a $1 billion in assets financial institution (FI) than a $500 million in assets FI.

Because it is intuitive, doesn't make it so. Over the course of the past 10 years, the number of FDIC-insured FIs decreased by 23% (see chart). The average asset size per institution increased from $753 million to $1.7 billion. Clearly, part of this consolidation wave was attributable to FIs striving for economies of scale and positive operating leverage.

(dollars in millions)	2000	2010	Change
Number of Institutions	9,904	7,657	-22.7%
Industry Assets	$7,462,898	$13,321,383	78.5%
Assets per Institution	$753.5	$1,739.8	130.9%

Source: FDIC

Has this consolidation, partly designed to give surviving institutions scale so they can spread relatively fixed costs over a larger franchise, resulted in positive operating leverage? My research into the subject says no.

One measure of achieving positive operating leverage is the efficiency ratio, defined as operating expense divided by the result of net interest income plus fee income. The lower the efficiency ratio, the greater the profitability. As an institution grows and is able to spread costs over a larger base, the efficiency ratio should go down.

But over the past ten years, efficiency ratios have risen in every asset category in both banks and thrifts with the exception of the very largest (>$10B in assets) banks (see charts).

US Bank Efficiency Ratio Trends

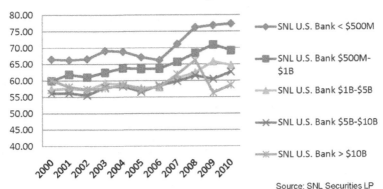

Source: SNL Securities LP

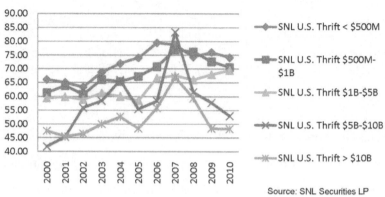

Source: SNL Securities LP

The efficiency ratio measures how much in operating expense it takes to generate a dollar of revenue. So what if revenues (net interest margin, or fee income) are on the decline? Naturally, the efficiency ratio will go up. To further isolate expenses, I reviewed how expense ratios, defined as operating expenses divided by average assets, fared for our industry (see chart).

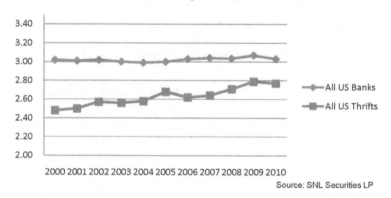

Source: SNL Securities LP

For banks, expense ratios have not budged during the period that resulted in a 23% reduction in FIs. Thrift expense ratios rose materially. I reviewed my company's bank and thrift product profitability reports to see if operating expenses per account declined during the 2000-2010 period. The answer: not one spread product group showed a decline in annualized cost per account. Not one.

Let's look at a couple of highly acquisitive FIs to see if they are achieving positive operating leverage by growing their balance sheets through mergers.

Fifth Third Bancorp

Fifth Third Bancorp is a $110 billion in assets financial institution with 1,363 branches and is headquartered in Cincinnati, Ohio. It has made six acquisitions totaling $32.6 billion in acquired assets between 2000 and 2007. The largest acquisition by far was the second quarter 2001 acquisition of Old Kent Financial, a $22.5 billion in assets bank. I chose this period to offset any impact from the 2008-2009 financial crisis. Clearly Fifth Third undertook acquisitions to achieve economies of scale. Relevant statistics during this period include:

	Total Assets ($000)	Efficiency Ratio (%)	Non-interest Expense/ AA (%)	EPS ($)
2000	45,856,906	50.80	2.52	1.83
2001	71,026,340	50.83	3.71	1.70
2002	80,899,212	46.24	2.96	2.59
2003	91,143,023	46.86	2.79	2.87
2004	94,455,731	53.64	3.18	2.68
2005	105,225,054	51.38	2.84	2.77
2006	100,669,263	54.46	2.92	2.13
2007	110,961,509	56.69	3.23	1.98

Source: SNL Securities LP

While Fifth Third's assets grew at a compound annual growth rate (CAGR) of 13.5%, earnings per share grew at a 1.1% CAGR and both the efficiency and expense ratios were higher in 2007 than when the bank was $45 billion in assets in 2000. Positive operating leverage should result in EPS growing faster than asset size because adding the next $100 in assets should cost less than the previous $100. Has Fifth Third achieved positive operating leverage by more than doubling the size of the bank during the measurement period?

BB&T

BB&T is a $157 billion in assets financial institution with 1,791 branches headquartered in Winston-Salem, North Carolina. It made 21 acquisitions totaling $44.6 billion in acquired assets from 2000 through 2007. BB&T acquired more, and often smaller, financial institutions during the measurement period than Fifth Third. Relevant statistics include:

	Total Assets ($000)	Efficiency Ratio (%)	Non-interest Expense/ AA (%)	EPS ($)
2000	59,340,228	50.41	3.41	1.53
2001	70,869,945	48.80	3.37	2.12
2002	80,216,816	50.76	3.16	2.72
2003	90,466,613	60.04	3.65	2.07
2004	100,508,641	49.75	3.02	2.80
2005	109,169,759	50.54	3.00	3.00
2006	121,351,065	52.83	3.05	2.81
2007	132,617,601	51.57	2.87	3.14

BB&T Corp

Source: SNL Securities LP

While BB&T's assets grew at a CAGR of 12.2%, earnings per share grew at 10.8%. But the efficiency ratio remained relatively steady in spite of BB&T's net interest margin falling from 4.20% in 2000 to 3.46% in 2007. The expense ratio declined, realizing economies of scale from its asset growth. Although EPS did not exceed asset growth, the culprit lies more in revenue generation than on realizing efficiencies from growth.

This analysis is a simple undertaking to determine if your financial institution is getting the results you want when executing a growth strategy to achieve economies of scale and positive operating leverage. If your results more closely resemble Fifth Third's than BB&T's, you should ask yourself why.

Economies of scale should result in lower efficiency and expense ratios, and greater profitability… i.e. positive operating leverage. If you are growing to spread relatively fixed costs over a greater revenue base, then you should measure to determine if you are succeeding. Success should result in better results to peer, industry benchmarks, and downward trends in operating costs per account. Growing absent success in these metrics means you are simply managing a more complex organization for no additional benefit.

Do you measure and hold yourself accountable for reducing relative costs as you grow?

~ Jeff

∞

Glacier Bancorp, Inc., a high performing bank holding company based in Kalispell, Montana, is a favorite of mine. At the end of 2019 it had an ROA of 1.64 percent and an ROE of 12.01 percent. It had $13.7 billion in total assets at that time. For as long as I've followed Glacier, its management has never failed to put up great numbers.

But there is a challenge. Five years prior, the bank's efficiency ratio was 52 percent and expense ratio was 2.60 percent. Total assets then were $8.3 billion. By the end of 2019 Glacier's efficiency ratio had crept up to 55 percent with a 2.82 percent expense ratio. What happened?

They had consolidated their 11 bank charters into one for efficiency. But that happened in 2012. So it likely had no impact. They completed eight mergers during the 2014-19 period, which stoked asset, loan, and deposit growth, while stunting tangible book-value-per-share growth. Most bank mergers—as a result of paying a price premium for the target—cause immediate tangible book-value-per-share dilution for the buyer upon completion.

However, the purpose of bank mergers is to achieve earnings-per-share growth more quickly than the bank could organically. The strategy is to buy the target, get the cost savings, and stoke further growth with your operating model. In the short term, however, this approach might inhibit positive operating leverage. The ultimate goal is to accelerate it. That takes discipline.

For the past five years, Glacier grew its assets at a 10.5 percent compound annual growth rate (CAGR), net loans at a 16.5 percent CAGR, and deposits at 11.2 percent. Earnings per share grew at a 9.5 percent CAGR and tangible book value per share at 5.7 percent for the same measurement period. But although Glacier maintained top-tier financial performance, it has not realized positive operating leverage during that time. (More recent quarterly performance is promising.)

So what has been holding things up for Glacier's operating leverage?

Bear in mind, equity investors could reasonably expect a 10 percent annual total return from a mature, conservatively run financial institution. Assuming the company's price-to-earnings ratio remains the same, a 9.5 percent earnings-per-share growth rate should equate to a 9.5 percent capital appreciation rate per year for the last five years. Combine that with a 3.4 percent dividend yield and you are likely to have happy investors. So I wouldn't get too caught up in the relatively slow tangible-book-value-per-share growth. As previously mentioned, Glacier completed eight mergers in five years, likely causing tangible book value dilution with each transaction. And they pay dividends—which by their nature stunt tangible book growth.

There is another headwind that might be at play: the law of large numbers. In banking, the law of large numbers means that as an institution grows, it takes tremendous organizational resources to replace the increased volume of loans that amortize and periodically pay off. It is common for a commercial bank to amortize or mature 20 percent of its loan book per year. A bank with $9.6 billion in loans would have to generate $1.9 billion in new loan originations just to hold serve. To grow 10 percent, the bank would have to originate $2.9 billion. That would take 146 lenders, each generating $20 million in annual production. Bigger banks go upstream for larger loan deals because of this very problem. Larger loan deals tend to be commodity priced, delivering lower net interest margins. The result: balance sheet growth exceeds earnings growth. And the challenge gets bigger.

Through strategic planning, bank executives may determine that they can't achieve growth and positive operating leverage to grow long-term earnings per share that would be satisfactory to shareholders. If so, then perhaps it is time to flip the switch from operating as a growth company to a cash cow. One that delivers an acceptable total return to investors, but does so with a greater proportion of that return coming in the form of dividends versus earnings growth. Glacier certainly has the financial performance and capital to make such a move. My guess is that they are poised to generate slower balance sheet growth and accelerate earnings growth through positive operating leverage. They have proven themselves in the past. Their credibility will likely result in shareholder patience.

To inject that level of discipline into your own operating philosophy, consider how your bank prioritizes three cultural values: transparency, long-term thinking, and leadership.

Transparency

So often I hear companies touting growth as the ultimate objective. Not just in banking, but other industries too. Grow or die is a common bromide. The key, of course, is to deliver returns to your stakeholders without straying from your organization's stated vision, markets, and risk appetite. Returning to our Glacier example, what if the executive team pursues a growth strategy—both organically and through acquisition—up until the point at which that pace of growth is no longer consistent with their mission? If the growth objective was earnings growth versus balance sheet growth—as it should be—then the bank can pursue positive operating leverage. In that context, it's perfectly respectable to grow the balance sheet at 5 percent, earnings per share at 7.5 percent, and to pay a 2.5 percent dividend yield. To meet shareholder expectations, however, you'll need to be transparent about the nature of your growth strategy.

I should re-emphasize that pursuing earnings growth need not benefit shareholders alone. Banks have multiple stakeholders, after all. Employees, through bonuses for a job well done, could also benefit. Customers may enjoy a bonus dividend on their core deposits, or a loan special just for them. And communities could benefit from the increased support of a financial institution that performs well as a result of its moderate balance sheet growth combined with positive operating leverage.

But the ultimate transition from a fast-growth strategy to a moderate one should be transparent to stakeholders. That goes particularly for employees tasked with executing the strategy and shareholders who might be rewarded differently. Constantly harping on a "growth" strategy without transparency into how that might transpire sets up the risk of disappointment. So be transparent about such an evolution.

The Long View

Financial institutions add capacity in chunks. They grow the balance sheet until resources are stretched, overtime goes up, and more mistakes get made. Then they go out and buy capacity in the form of employees, technology, or fixed assets so they can grow until they are stretched again. During that immediate time after purchasing capacity, efficiency and expense ratios will likely go up. That's not consistent with generating positive operating leverage.

Capacity planning for financial institutions is challenging compared to industries that have repeatable processes, like manufacturing. In banking, process breakages can cause frequent interruptions. When underwriting a credit, for example, the credit analyst may have to request information from the borrower and then wait to receive it. Also, the method for measuring capacity might be different in each functional area. In credit, you might measure how many loans the most productive analyst underwrites versus the least productive. Or how many loans were processed during peak demand. Was there overtime during that period? Were there cars in the parking lot at 6:00 p.m.?

Once department managers assess capacity and compare it to the growth strategy, it might be time to either: 1) Review processes and existing technology to try to increase capacity without adding resources. 2) Look into buying additional capacity. If you go with the second option, then the cost of your department—let's say it's the deposit operations department—will go up in the short run as a percent of total deposits. Ultimately, that investment should result in a decreased operating-expense-to-deposits ratio. That is why bankers should take the long view in achieving positive operating leverage.

It's like race cars engaged in a 500-mile race, as mentioned in a prior chapter. They enter the pits several times. Why? It certainly doesn't help them win the race to pull off of the track. But if they didn't pull off the track, their tires would blow or they'd run out of gas. They enter the pits so they can win the 500-mile race. So too should bankers enter the pits to add capacity to achieve positive operating leverage. That should lead to improved financial performance.

Leadership

Implementing disciplined operating models that lead to positive operating leverage requires leadership. And while strong leaders will bring transparency and long-term thinking to an organization, they will also make tough decisions and take accountability for the results. They will also demand accountability from management and staff at every level. Leadership, as a cultural value within the organization, means that these qualities are rewarded, not punished, at the bank.

Of course, the short-term approach—managing by budget—is easier and more expedient than playing the long game. The challenge is that, all things being equal, the time never seems quite right to add capacity that will cause you to temporarily regress. However, many financial institutions that follow this short-term operating model run out of gas and end up looking for partners that can remediate the infrastructure they have routinely neglected. What kind of leadership does that reflect?

Generating positive operating leverage also calls for a broader perspective on how to invest and how to ensure that the investment provides value to the bank. For example, many banks require a return on investment analysis when marketing or front-line bankers propose a new product or technology. But what about the loan servicing department's investment in tax payment tracking? Suppose that subscribing to such a service drives up your loan servicing operating costs as a percent of loans from 15 basis points to 16 basis points. Sound like a poor move? What if it allows the bank to grow real estate loans without adding personnel—ultimately driving down costs to 13 basis points as a percent of loans in year three? Would you do it then? The key is, when the decision is made to make the investment, the department manager is responsible for driving down those costs, long-term. In that sense, isn't that manager delivering an ROI?

Multi-year discipline at this level can't be accomplished without leadership. Maintain accountability, and when department managers deliver on the promise, they should be rewarded appropriately. And publicly. Build a culture in which those types of successes are replicated by others. That's leadership, and it nurtures discipline in executing the business model that generates positive operating leverage.

To Sum It Up...

As you grow, it should cost less to generate the next $100 million in assets and the next $100 in revenue. But that doesn't mean it has to happen every year. Over the long-term—defined as the amount of time it takes to realize the full economic benefit of your current strategy—growth should result in lower efficiency and expense ratios. Operating leverage is the basis of economies of scale. Yet many financial institutions are challenged to achieve it. If it seems you're never big enough, maybe you're asking the wrong question. Maybe you should ask whether you're disciplined enough.

Points Made This Chapter

❖ It is common for growing financial institutions to struggle to achieve positive operating leverage.

❖ Bankers should be transparent to their stakeholders in how they approach growth and efficiency.

❖ Financial institutions should "enter the pits" to increase capacity. This requires a long-term view of financial performance.

❖ The success of strategic investments to increase capacity can be measured. But it may take more than next year's budget to realize the benefits.

❖ Leadership and discipline are required in building a culture that reduces relative costs long-term.

Chapter 7

Why Do Banks Merge?

Why do banks merge? Economy of scale is the obvious answer. Yet the cynic inside your head might suspect the motive is the same as that of a childless couple that buys a McMansion or a debutante that buys a Bentley. Remember when NationsBank and First Union Bank tried to outdo each other by occupying progressively taller towers in Charlotte, North Carolina? Wasn't it a sight flying into the Charlotte airport to see the manifestation of Hugh McColl's and Ed Crutchfield's egos dominate the skyline?

Fast forward a few decades to witness the latest landmark move by banking titans. This time, it won't involve a skyline duel. Instead, Kelly King, BB&T's CEO, and Bill Rogers, Suntrust's leader, are taking their toys in Winston-Salem and Atlanta, respectively, and building a bigger boat in Charlotte together. The $30.8 billion deal, announced in 2018 and completed in 2019, created the sixth largest bank in the country at the time the deal closed. An *American Banker* interview let the leaders tell the story in their own words:[xxiv]

Rogers: The fun part about the building is that it's a blank canvass, which is exciting as we think about how people work together. It is an ability to create something new.

King: We started out with a concept of how we thought banking would play out in the new world. We found out through lots and lots of dialogue that the concept is proving to be reality, which is really exciting.

Rogers: There's a great level of excitement and a great level of looking forward to making [systems] choices. There are very few opportunities in a career to do that. It has created a spring in everybody's step.

King: As we talked more with teammates about our T3 strategy [which focuses on personal touch, technology and trust to gain clients] we found out that not only did it resonate with them but it gets them excited.

Clearly, they were excited. And why shouldn't they be? What they're really talking about is the ability to create greater economies of scale. To deliver that positive operating leverage so elusive to many financial institutions that merge. To have more money to spend on technology to compete with the big five.

Why did so many readers gravitate toward my take on this particular merger? It's tied to their interest in generating positive operating leverage. Is there some secret sauce to building a grand financial institution that masters technology, employee engagement, and the customer experience—while delivering superior shareholder returns? Could BB&T and Suntrust find it? Here is what I wrote.

∞

Why Suntrust and BB&T? Why?

February 11, 2019

https://www.jeff4banks.com/2019/02/why-suntrust-and-bb.html

I know on the investor conference call, Kelly King of BB&T and Bill Rogers of SunTrust spoke to why. But I may not have been listening well.

I suppose much of the discussion revolved around scale. So, along with my first inclination, my second inclination was also... why?

The Numbers

Here are their slash lines (read: Assets/ROA/ROE/5-Year Annual EPS Growth/Dividend Yield)

BBT: $225B / 1.47% / 10.95% / 9.5% / 3.3%

STI: $216B / 1.34% / 11.50% / 15.5% / 3.1%

BBT (bank only) had $6.3B in operating expenses in 2018, five percent of which is in the Call Report category "Data Processing Expense", defined as expenses paid for data processing and equipment such as telephones and modems. It does not include employees. STI (bank only) had $5.4B, 10% of which was in Data Processing Expense. I find it difficult to believe they can't find enough money in that pot or outside of the Data Processing pot for technology innovation. It would be a travesty of management.

Perhaps they would find it difficult to maintain that level of EPS growth, given the law of large numbers. But they chose to solve that problem by becoming larger? BB&T will issue 1.295 shares for each SunTrust share outstanding, increasing their share count from 777 million to 1.4 billion. So to earn one cent per share more, the combined company would have to generate $14 million in additional net income. And at the 1.5% ROA BB&T already achieves, they would have to grow $933 million for each penny of EPS growth. To maintain 10% EPS growth, the combined bank would have to grow about $39 billion per year (42 cents x $933MM).

Perhaps they felt the pressure "to do something", as my BB&T regional business banker friend told me, saying that at their size they were in "no man's land". I don't know what that means. But an investment banker told me today that investors are intolerant of tangible book value per share dilution of more than three years. So if you feel you need to "do something", and can't overly dilute your book value, perhaps a merger of equals (MOE) makes sense.

I have preached MOE virtues for banks that could actually benefit from scale to achieve better efficiency ratios. Statistically, banks between $5B and $10B in total assets are better at it than larger financial institutions. But I digress.

Law of Large Numbers

I have written in the past about financial institutions running into the law of large numbers, leaving only acquisition as its means to meet shareholder expectations. I'm not saying it's impossible, as JPMorgan Chase did it ($2.6T in total assets, 14% EPS CAGR since 2014). But it's difficult. And JPM received a huge boost from tax cuts.

Financial institutions, in my experience, are not keen on turning themselves into cash cows, maximizing their profitability with slower growth and paying a higher proportion of shareholder returns in dividends. Financial institutions also don't tend to buy and divest lines of business as a means to stoke shareholder returns, as very large industrial firms do (i.e. GE).

So if BB&T and SunTrust have ample operating budgets to invest in technology, and are delivering strong shareholder returns, in good markets.. i.e. almost the same markets...

I ask: Why merge?

~ Jeff

∞

This isn't a BB&T and Suntrust story. And for the record, the combined bank changed its name to Truist. This is a story about discipline. Discipline in identifying and fostering a positive accountability culture, discipline in developing employees to manage and lead as the bank grows, and discipline in developing strategy to remain an important partner in the future of your stakeholders. In other words, to build a scalable business model.

Mergers involve risk. You are putting two cultures together. Read publicly available merger press releases. Whether the merger involves financial institutions or companies in any other industry, merger partners commonly refer to culture as an important component to successful integration. But you start behind the eight ball, because the employees of the acquired firm know the ax is coming. How else do buyers earn back the premium they pay for the target?

The larger the partner, the more challenging it is to impact culture. Wells Fargo had been under a consent order for years because of its fake account debacle. Among other scandals, the bank incented branch employees to achieve eight products per customer and designed its accountability culture around achieving this goal, regardless of customer need. That cost two CEOs their jobs, and it is taking years to turn around the toxic culture they unknowingly created. Because they are so big. It's more like turning an aircraft carrier than a speed boat. So if your merger partner is large—and has an undesirable culture or some unintended consequences from cultural negligence—that will likely spread to the buyer.

In other words, there is a reason why a seller decides to sell. Be diligent in uncovering it. A merger can make sense for a number of reasons. Economies of scale, succession, competitor elimination, new markets and products, and bridging the strategy/value gap are the most compelling.

Accounting for Economies of Scale

We covered economies of scale, as a concept, in the previous chapter, "Positive Operating Leverage." It's worth noting here, though, that if you merge to achieve economies of scale, make sure you build accountabilities into your post-merger operations. I reviewed three of the largest merger transactions in 2016: Huntington Bancshares/First Merit, Old National Bancorp/Anchor BanCorp Wisconsin, and First Interstate BancSystem/Cascade Bancorp. The respective buyers said the following in their merger press releases:

"We are very pleased to come together with FirstMerit to create a regional bank with added customer convenience, an enhanced portfolio of products for consumers and businesses, as well as strong market share."
~ Stephen Steinour, Huntington's chairman, president and CEO

"This partnership … is a natural extension of our franchise and our growth strategy." Not only does it position Old National in strong, vibrant markets with proven growth potential, it also represents an exceptional cultural fit and an opportunity to continue the strong legacy of service that distinguishes AnchorBank."
~ Bob Jones, Old National's president and CEO

"The transaction is expected to generate 8% earnings accretion in 2018, taking into account the cap on interchange fees. Over the longer term the deal should boost profit by 10% annually."
~ First Interstate press release

In the three years after the merger, Huntington achieved a 12 percent compound annual growth rate (CAGR) in earnings per share compared to the year prior to the merger announcement. Interstate achieved a 10 percent CAGR, and Old National an 8 percent CAGR for the same period. If Interstate achieved the 10 percent profit boost claimed by its merger press release, the bank must have been projecting zero percent organic EPS growth. When merging, be transparent about what you mean by achieving economies of scale and maintain accountabilities to achieve it.

Solving a Succession Issue, Eliminating a Competitor

In 2007, something terrible happened. The CEO of First Columbia Bank and Trust in Bloomsburg, Pennsylvania passed away suddenly. And there was no successor at the bank. Bloomsburg is a small, slow-growing town in the middle of the state, fueled substantially by a university of the same name.

First Columbia had an in-town competitor, Columbia County Farmers National Bank (CCFNB). A mouthful of a name. The banks were friendly, yet competitive. Both were relatively small, about $325 million in total assets each, and they both competed with large banks and other community banks in Bloomsburg and the surrounding towns. It would've made sense for them to merge prior to the CEO's passing. But it never happened.

When First Columbia's board began assessing the alternatives, they decided to seriously consider merging with their cross-town rival. But they wouldn't do it unless they could assess the abilities of CCFNB's CEO and conclude that they would be willing to hire him as their CEO. So they approached the potential merger like a CEO search, calling him in to be interviewed by a committee of the board.

As it happened, succession was First Columbia's reason for considering something that it had not considered before. But as board members assessed their strategic alternatives, they realized they needed greater scale to pay for escalating technology costs. Without that, it would only get harder to compete with the very large financial institutions and even some of the larger community banks in their market. Eliminating a rival was another benefit to the combination. They could join forces to be a more formidable foe.

And so they did. Today, that bank has a 1.14 percent ROA and an 8.58 percent ROE. The ROE could be higher if the bank didn't carry so much "E" in the form of a tangible equity/assets ratio of 11.67 percent. And it pays a 4 percent dividend yield on its stock. So, although I would not consider this bank to be very big at its current $820 million in total assets, it is big enough to deliver that level of profit in small town America. Although succession drove the merger, both institutions benefitted from greater economies of scale and one less competitor. The new CEO says it was one of the best moves either bank ever made.

Acquiring New Products, Entering New Markets

Byline Bank is a Chicagoland commercial bank that was in serious regulatory hot water in 2013 when an investor group recapitalized it, consolidated multiple bank charters, and dug it out of trouble. In June 2016, Byline announced its acquisition of Ridgestone Bank, which had grown to become a national leading Small Business Administration lender, consistently ranking as one of the Top 10 SBA lenders in the country.

For Ridgestone, the deal was about funding—it had only two branches—and product diversification. At the time the transaction was announced, Ridgestone's CEO said that the challenges of running a monoline business with limited branches proved challenging, and Byline was an attractive partner. For Byline, CEO Alberto Paracchini said, "it was an attractive product segment." He added: "It's something that we feel we needed to have in our suite of products to offer to our basic commercial banking customers."[xxv] So Byline's motivation was to acquire new products—i.e., SBA lending—and to enter new markets, i.e., diversify its dependence on Chicagoland with a national presence.

In the year prior to the Ridgestone acquisition, Byline Bank lost $12 million as it continued with its rebuilding. In the year after the transaction closed, it made $25 million. But Byline wasn't done adding products and business lines via acquisition. In late 2017, Byline announced the acquisition of Evanston, Illinois-based First Evanston Bancorp. On the surface, this might have appeared as an in-market consolidation. But it was more.

In 2016, Byline Bank only had 19 percent of its loan portfolio in commercial and industrial loans. First Evanston had 35 percent. By doing the acquisition, Byline became a much more significant business lender. That's something community financial institutions frequently talk about, even as they remain addicted to commercial real estate lending. Today, Byline has no such addiction, with a loan portfolio that is 51 percent real estate—mostly commercial real estate—and 41 percent business loans.

Bridging the Strategy/Value Gap

Another compelling reason for entering into a merger, bridging a strategy/value gap, also merits discussion. A strategy/value gap is the difference between the value you can reasonably expect to receive if you were bought by another financial institution compared to the present value of your strategy.

There are some caveats, of course. Caveat one is that by not selling, your institution retains the right to sell. That has option value. And much like a stock option, there is a present value in retaining that option. Secondly, if your institution serves a higher purpose, and places equal value in how you serve all stakeholders, your board might be more tolerant of a slightly greater strategy value gap than a bank that is indifferent to other stakeholders. In other words, in addition to shareholders, your institution matters to employees, customers, and communities. At least more so than it does to a would-be buyer.

The strategy/value gap concept was hammered home at the end of a strategic planning process I moderated, when the CEO asked his management team: "Is this the best we could do?" The management team did not think the bank could achieve faster EPS growth. And the CEO knew that the plan would not deliver enough value to satisfy the directors, who represent the shareholders.

In the ensuing year, this bank aggressively pursued a merger target to try to bridge the strategy/value gap with an accretive deal. That transaction became too pricey and went to a competitor. And that competitor, as it turned out, overpaid for it. With reduced capital levels, and therefore an insufficient buffer to defend against recession, the competitor ended up selling in a weakened condition.

The bank with the strategy/value gap could not bridge it and ended up selling as well. Financial institutions should build aspirational strategic plans for this very reason. Not unachievable. But not overly conservative. If you build a plan that the management team is very, very, very comfortable it can achieve, you are likely building a large strategy/value gap into the plan. Even if the board and management preach serving all stakeholders equally, this does not mean "at the expense of shareholders." The strategy/value gap may be so large that the board rejects the plan and becomes suspicious of management's capabilities. Or the board may decide to sell the bank because of the huge divide between the present value of the sand-bagged strategy and what the bank could reasonably achieve in a sale. Bankers should mind the gap.

To Sum It Up...

Mergers should not be about ego. And yet, we might not be shocked to see a merger press release that quotes the buyer's CEO as saying: "I have an enormous ego and I think I'm a better banker than [Bank XYZ's CEO], but their bank is bigger than mine and I had to do something about it." Deep down, we sometimes believe this is the primary reason some mergers happen. Economy of scale is certainly a legitimate reason to merge. But what is the right scale to spread fixed costs across a larger base—and make the necessary technology and talent development investments—to remain relevant in a changing environment? It might not be as big as some would have us think..

Points Made This Chapter

❖ Ego is not a legitimate reason to merge.

❖ If you are delivering excellent financial performance with solid shareholder returns while making significant technology investments, why merge?

❖ Mergers involve operational and cultural risk.

❖ Legitimate reasons to merge include: economies of scale or critical mass; elimination of a competitor; succession; entry into new markets or acquisition of new products; and bridging a strategy/value gap.

❖ There is a reason why a seller decides to sell. Be diligent in uncovering it.

❖ Be transparent on what you mean by economies of scale and financial targets for a merger. Be accountable for achieving them.

❖ The strategy/value gap is the difference between what you can reasonably achieve in a sale and the present value of your strategy. Mind the gap.

Chapter 8

Charters, Divisions, or One Brand?

In 2012 Glacier Bank announced it would consolidate its 11 bank charters into one, and in 2015 Zions Bank elected to do the same with its seven charters. Were these high-profile consolidations the death knell of the multi-charter approach?

Maybe. Aside from having multiple examinations from different regulators, each bank has its own policies and procedures. Another issue is that capital does not move efficiently among the banks under the holding company. One bank has to dividend up to the holding company, which in turn downstreams the funds to the other bank. If the regulators permit it, that is. In difficult times, regulators will restrict dividends being upstreamed from a bank because they want the capital *in* the bank.

Maintaining multiple charters comes with other challenges as well: Holding company support centers require a separate contract for each bank they serve, and the ability to upstream to the holding company to pay the bills. If one bank has excess liquidity, it's limited in its ability to shore up liquidity in the other bank. Managing interest rate risk for the whole company is also difficult. As a result, the multi-charter approach has fallen out of favor.

But what about running several brands under a single charter?

In the past, conventional wisdom advised against sponsoring two or more brands at one financial institution—either through unique charters or as separate divisions of one chartered bank. Systems limitations, financial reporting, and advertising/branding inefficiencies were the most common reasons to avoid this strategy. Radio and television markets are large, the thinking went, so why build multiple brands or run a checking account campaign for one brand and not another? Wouldn't that double the cost?

The question is whether this logic holds true today. Sure, television markets are still large. However, modernized systems can now handle multiple divisions. Financial reporting has improved to separate the profit performance of each. And with the advent of digital advertising and content-driven brand building, the traditional advertising and media market argument is also weaker. Much weaker.

Glacier must have thought so. Including its flagship brand—Glacier Bank—it now supports 16 brands across Montana, Idaho, Washington, Wyoming, Colorado, Arizona, Utah, and Nevada.[xxvi] It's worth noting that many of these brands are within close proximity of one another. Glacier has a First Bank and a First State Bank in Wyoming, which has a population of 580,000! So no, Glacier isn't buying the argument against multiple brands.

Also worth noting: Glacier Bancorp's ROA was 1.64 percent and its ROE was 12.01 percent. What does it take to succeed with multiple divisions as Glacier has?

Clearly, many bankers want to find out. More and more affinity brands have been popping up, and others are certainly in consideration at strategic planning sessions. My first take on the topic generated a lot of interest within the industry. Here's what I had to say.

∞

Schmidlap Bank, A Division of Community Bank

November 4, 2017

https://www.jeff4banks.com/2017/11/schmidlap-bank-division-of-community.html

"We want to keep our charter because the OCC is a more distinguished regulator." Seriously, that is what a bank chairman told me when arguing to keep his bank's charter during merger negotiations.

But I try not to judge. Perhaps, if I thought the argument weak, which I did, there was something else behind it. Something like "we've spent 100 years building the reputation of this bank and 'poof', it's gone at the stroke of a pen." Or, "my grandparents, parents, and now me served on the board of this bank and I owe it to their legacy..."

Why not just say that? Perhaps there is little evidence of the benefit of your 100-year brand, so it's a difficult argument to make. But more difficult than claiming the OCC is a better regulator?

In more recent merger discussions, however, I have heard more refreshing arguments that it is not necessary to re-brand every nook and cranny of your bank into one. Because one key argument to combine brands is the efficiency of advertising into one or more media markets. Does this make sense today?

I think not. Take the accompanying picture, all from my Twitter, Facebook, and LinkedIn streams. Three different "promoted" posts. All specific to me. Based on all the intel gathered on me. My neighbor, or even my wife, see different ads. So combining names so you can realize synergies in your billboard strategy doesn't make sense like it did 20 years ago.

Pick what you want, to get what you need.

amazon

More success stories of the divisional approach are cropping up in our industry. One of my favorites is the affinity brand Redneck Bank, a division of All America Bank. All America Bank is a traditional community bank located near Oklahoma City, and has been around since the 1960's. And yes, they recently switched names from Bank of the Witchitas. But did they have to? For the traditional bank, I'm not so sure.

Aside from the traditional bank, they thought out of the box, and established a digital-only division to appeal to a specific niche. And it has done well. Marvelously well. Even though it has not reached the "critical mass" that your investment bankers insist that you need. See the accompanying table.

	At or for Quarter Ended September 30, 2017		
	$250MM-$500MM	USNY Bank	All America Bank
Total Assets ($000)	342,733	348,798	404,346
ROAA (%)	0.98	1.32	1.18
ROAE (%)	8.83	13.11	10.32
Net Interest Margin (%)	3.63	4.05	4.30
Efficiency Ratio (%)	67.96	44.24	66.33
Non-interest Expense/AA (%)	2.82	1.92	3.15

Source: S&P Global Market Intelligence

On a more traditional front, I point to USNY Bank in upstate New York. This bank, unlike All America Bank, is relatively new, having been formed in 2007. Its strategy, however, is to build brands that resonate closer to the communities where they operate. For example, the $349 million bank has only four branch locations, each USNY Bank. But they operate as Bank of the Finger Lakes, or Bank of Cooperstown, divisions of USNY. Their financial performance doesn't seem to be hampered by bifurcated branding.

The divisional approach is becoming more important as relatively small financial institutions worry about keeping up with customer preference, technology, and regulatory changes. Although I mock the investment banker that always seems to think your institution needs to be twice the size you are now, regardless of the size you are now, there is merit to achieving a certain size.

Merits that include: increased stock trading multiples, greater employee development opportunities, the ability to absorb regulatory costs, and greater resources to invest in technologies to afford you a long-term future.

But you need not give up your name to get a merger of like-sized institutions done. Nor dump your local brand for a homogeneous one that spans geographies.

~ Jeff

∞

To succeed at running more than one bank brand under a single umbrella, you have to be clear on exactly what you're trying to accomplish. Making a merger happen has been one common reason for keeping multiple charters. The "100-year history" argument resonates strongly with many boards of directors and management teams. Few want to be recommending a merger in which their storied financial institution gets merged into oblivion. Buyers willing to do the multi-charter approach have had an advantage among the universe of sellers. Merge with us, keep your bank.

And many multi-charter bank holding companies remain. However, the spate of high-profile charter consolidations weakens the appeal. Once merged, the holding company board can elect to do what Glacier and Zions did.

Absent this advantage, why maintain separate brands? There are a few likely answers: to serve a niche constituency; to patch balance sheet and profitability holes without disintermediating your customers or repricing the balance sheet; to boost revenue by partnering with non-banks; and to expand beyond the traditional geographic footprint, to name a few. Consider whether these objectives make sense for your institution. Then determine whether pursuing them requires a separate charter—with all of the disadvantages mentioned earlier—or whether a divisional approach will serve the purpose.

Serve a Niche

A Pennsylvania bank I once worked with had a solid lending machine, but a challenged branch network. It operated with low levels of liquidity and a relatively high loan-to-deposit ratio. Because the bank's strategy was to attract funding via price, it also suffered from a high cost of funds compared to its peer banks.

I suggested something a bit outside the box. Mobile banking was in its infancy at the time, and online banking was becoming increasingly accepted. The idea was for the bank to start an affinity division for local churches, in which the church would receive credit for the average deposit balances of the congregation.

It was a variation on the concept of affinity credit cards, which have been around for decades. Think of airline credit cards. They still have representatives chasing you down at airports. Why are airlines so interested in co-branding a credit card? To get a piece of the revenue stream. And why are airline customers interested having a co-branded airline card? To get free travel. So why not have an affinity church division that gives the church a piece of the revenue stream, and satisfies the congregations' desire to increase funding to their churches? The answer to that, of course, depends on the mission and culture of the bank in question (and the churches in its market area). The idea went over like a lead balloon.

That bank later sold. But the idea of serving area churches with a division of your bank is an example of serving a specific niche.

Fitness Bank, a nationwide division of Affinity Bank in Covington, Georgia, is an online lifestyle bank serving customers with an interest in physical fitness and financial strength. The bank rewards customers for being active. The more steps they take and log into their online portal or app, the higher the interest rate received on their Fitness Savings Account. The bank's website, in addition to content relating to fitness, has a step leaderboard of its customers.

Affinity Bank recently converted from a mutual to a stock form of ownership. And the Fitness Bank division came to Affinity by way of a 2019 acquisition. There wasn't much public disclosure on the size of the division relative to the rest of the bank. Proper experimentation and execution will be important to its future success.

A more seasoned niche bank division is the previously-mentioned Redneck Bank, a division of All America Bank. This online-only bank division started in 2008, around the same time that I recommended the church division to the Pennsylvania banker. What, exactly, is the niche? The CEO told the American Bankers Association's *ABA Banking Journal* that the brand targeted "people with a sense of humor."[xxvii] Sure. Or, maybe, it's the contrarians around the country who wear what some may deem to be a slur as a badge of honor.

Either way, more than 85 percent of All America Bank's deposit growth over the past five years occurred in its headquarters branch in Mustang, Oklahoma—where, presumably, Redneck Bank's deposits reside. The bank is not public so there is no enhanced disclosure or investor presentations other than Call Report filings with the FDIC. All America Bank had a 1.49 percent ROA and a 14.86 percent ROE.

Patch Balance Sheet and Profitability Holes

In 2006, Flushing Bank had a challenge. Headquartered in New York City—arguably the most competitive deposit market in the world—the bank had a loan-to-deposit ratio in excess of 130 percent. They were "loaned up."

The economy was strong at that time, and they had built a successful lending machine. Should they continue to fund it? If so, where should they get the funds? Expand their branch network? Tweak rates? Launch new products? Flushing's solution was to launch iGOBanking.com, an online-only brand specifically designed to provide another outlet for funding loans.

When calculating the incremental operating cost of the division—plus the interest expense offered to iGOBanking.com customers—is it more expensive than adding a branch? Consider all the factors at play. At that time, bank management said the intent of the division was to fund loan growth by gathering deposits *outside* New York and to allow branch employees to refocus on relationship building.[xxviii] Although supporting your balance sheet with price-driven funding may not add organizational value, it can plug holes. And because employees weren't saddled with opening accounts for local rate shoppers, they had more time to focus on relationship building. After launch, and prior to the financial crisis, the bank's loan-to-deposit ratio fell to 119 percent. Still high, but not uncommon for New York City financial institutions.

Generate Revenue from Non-Banks Masquerading as Banks

"Banking that has your back." So says the marketing collateral for Chime, a neo-bank that would have you believe it is an actual bank—unless you scroll to the bottom of its homepage or open an account.

Chime's mission, according to its website: "We created Chime because we believe everyone deserves financial peace of mind. We're building a new kind of online bank account that helps members get ahead by making managing money easy. It's your money. It's your life. Chime in." Other homepage copy boasts fee-free overdrafts up to $100, the ability get paid up to two days before payday with direct deposit, no hidden fees, and automatic savings features.

In very small print at the bottom of Chime's homepage: "Banking services provided by The Bancorp Bank or Stride Bank, N.A., Members FDIC. The Chime Visa® Debit Card is issued by The Bancorp Bank or Stride Bank pursuant to a license from Visa U.S.A. Inc. and may be used everywhere Visa debit cards are accepted. The Chime Visa® Credit Builder Card is issued by Stride Bank pursuant to a license from Visa

U.S.A. Inc."

You may have never heard of The Bancorp Bank. If this is your first time seeing this bank's name, and you're thinking they didn't hire Interbrand to come up with it, join the crowd. (That might have proved to be a savvy cost savings move. Interbrand is the brain trust that came up with Truist.)

Bear in mind, The Bancorp Bank was not built to be an iconic retail brand. It was built to be a bank serving other financial services. Its payments solutions group, for example, supports such emerging brands as Betterment and Hyper wallet, a PayPal Service. It also supports Varo Money, which is moving its platform to the newly minted bank charter, Varo Bank, N.A.

These banking-as-a-service (BaaS) banks have company among traditional banks that operate BaaS divisions alongside their traditional community bank offerings. Sutton Bank in Attica, Ohio is a privately held community bank that focuses on small business and ag lending. It operates eight full-service branches throughout four counties in north-central Ohio. From the curbside view, it looks much like any other small Midwestern community bank.

But Sutton has an ace up its sleeve. It also operates as Sutton Payments, a division that provides prepaid card solutions to non-banks, much as The Bancorp Bank does. Sutton has issued hundreds of card programs for non-banks since its founding in 2000 and has transitioned from an issuing organization to a payments facilitator. Its most recent year's financial performance included an ROA of 3.11 percent and an ROE of 30.03 percent. Fully one-third of its total revenue was prepaid card fee income.

Expand Geographically

If you buy into the reasoning behind using bank divisions as a means to facilitate a merger, you'll also appreciate its corollary: the geographic expansion argument. The theory is that many local bank names don't translate well outside of their original region or branch network, and therefore, expanding markets call for multiple brands. I find this argument weak as a hard-and-fast rule. Umpqua Bank is named after an obscure Native American term for "near the river"—the bank's original location when it was founded in Canyonville, Oregon in 1953. Yet that name has prevailed as a superstar brand across the bank's current footprint in the Pacific Northwest, California, Idaho, and Nevada. And of course, the TD in TD Bank stands for Toronto Dominion, an association that has stuck, even as the bank has increased its dominion across the U.S.

On the other hand, using divisions to leverage the power of hyper-local branding can be an effective strategy, whether you're expanding through mergers or de novo branching. CNB Bank in Clearfield, Pennsylvania, provides a good case study. The town of Clearfield is the seat of the rural Pennsylvania county of the same name. It's so rural, in fact, that many PA residents may not know where it is. Pennsylvania has several counties that are considered a hunters' paradise, and Clearfield is one of them—and it has one of the largest gun and ammo shops in the state.

In 2005, CNB Bank eyed Erie, in northwest Pennsylvania, as an expansion market. And when it failed to acquire another bank there, it took a different tack. Instead of merging, it opened de novo branches in Erie. It hired a highly-connected team of bankers. And voila,

ERIEBANK, a division of CNB Bank, was formed. Today, the ERIEBANK division represents 28 percent of CNB Bank deposits.

CNB didn't stop there. In 2013, it acquired FC Bancorp in and around Columbus, Ohio—quite a distance from its existing footprint. Today, the FCBank division represents 11 percent of CNB Bank deposits. Then in 2016, CNB started another de novo division, similar to ERIEBANK, in Buffalo, New York. Its name: BankOnBuffalo. That division represents 29 percent of total bank deposits and 39 percent of its total deposit growth.

Have multiple divisions stunted CNB's financial performance? It's slash line (ROA/ROE/One-Year EPS Growth/5-Year Total Return to Shareholders):

1.19 percent/12.14 percent/19 percent/104 percent.

You be the judge.

To Sum It Up...

Running multiple divisions under your bank should not double your marketing spend. If it does, check the effectiveness of the marketing spend. Although a division does not preserve the 100-year old charter, it could preserve a 100-year tradition of customer support, employee satisfaction, and community building. It could also preserve an iconic local brand, even if that brand has merged with a larger neighbor to achieve the needed scale to continue serving those stakeholders into the future.

Points Made This Chapter

❖ Multi-charter bank holding companies have fallen out of favor because of the inefficiencies that result from multiple regulators and exams, and the difficulty in managing capital, liquidity, interest rate risk, and operations across several banks.

❖ Systems limitations, financial reporting, and advertising/branding inefficiencies are weak arguments against the divisional approach.

❖ Maintaining a bank's brand as a separate division could facilitate a merger in which the target is unwilling to give up what it perceives as a storied brand.

❖ Other reasons to form divisions of your financial institution: to serve a niche, to patch balance sheet and profitability holes, to execute a BaaS strategy, and promote geographic expansion.

Section III

Who Cares About Products and Marketing?

Determining why your target customers switch financial service providers assumes you know who your target customers are.

Chapter 9

Brand Value and Brand Equity:
How Do They Measure Up?

When bankers tell me their institution has a superior brand, I want to know what that means. Too often they believe they have a superior brand simply because customers come up to senior executives or board members on the street and tell them so. That's nice, but it doesn't mean much.

Brand is the connection of companies to their stakeholders. That's not a touchy-feely concept—you can, and should, wrap hard numbers around it. To measure your connection to customers, find out whether the brand merits higher price points, achieves deeper relationships, and/or leads to shorter sales cycles. To measure the brand's connection to employees, ask yourself: Do we fill positions quicker, attract top talent, and keep the keepers longer? Also consider your brand's connection to shareholders and local communities. Do surveys indicate that your institution is viewed as a point of light within your community? And do your shareholders award you higher trading multiples or perceive you as credible when implementing strategic bets that may have a longer payoff?

For consumer products, brand value can be intuitively measured. Like when my daughter did an unscientific blind taste test among soda brands at the local pool club. She compared Coke, Pepsi, RC, and the generic store brand. The generic brand won the most votes. And the price point was 40 percent cheaper than Coke and Pepsi. Yet those other two brands sell more. In this example, you could convincingly argue that the value of brand is the cost of the branded item minus the cost of the unbranded one, multiplied by the number of items sold.

Not so easy in financial institutions. Sure, banks can compare the interest rate paid by wholesale banks—such as Discover Bank—over their own current rates on similar products to determine their brand value. Or they can compare the lower yield on a loan accepted by wholesale lenders—such as insurance companies—on a commercial real estate deal. Someday, when those types of competitors are more prolific in your markets, this might be the most accurate way to do it. But for now, how does your brand compare to most of your competition—the national, regional, and local community financial institutions?

That question was the genesis of the bank brand value (BBV) calculation developed in the article below and visited by so many readers.

∞

Bank Brand Value: Calculated!

April 9, 2019

https://www.jeff4banks.com/2019/04/bank-brand-value-calculated.html

I ask and ask and ask: what does brand get you?

Does it get you pricing power, shorter sales cycles, better employees, more loyal customers? Or does it get you increased expenses without measurable results?

Forbes calculated brand value in their "World's Most Valuable Brands" by taking anything that a company achieves over an 8% return on equity.[xxix] Many people pay close attention to the ranking. Although I find the calculation to be arbitrary. What if the company is more capital intensive, and has to carry more capital than other companies? So the ROE is lower. Or what if a company is excellent at expense control? Driving ROE higher, but hardly due to its brand.

No, I do not like Forbes' calculation. It particularly doesn't work well for financial institutions. Which is probably why the first bank on their list is ranked 43rd. And it's Wells Fargo! Didn't help out Tim Sloan.

Bank Brand Value ("BBV")

So how would I calculate a financial institution's brand value? When I speak, I use great brand images such as Starbucks, JW Marriott, and Mercedes Benz. Why do these brands command higher price points than Dunkin, Best Western, and Kia?

Price points. A superior brand usually would command superior price points. And we can measure this by looking at a financial institution's cost of interest bearing deposits, and yield on loans, compared to other regional players that have similar balance sheets. Spread is usually 80%-85% of a community bank's revenues. An inferior or non-existent brand likely grows deposits and loans via decisions made in pricing committee.

Math

Fortunately, we have good data via Call Reports to make the calculation. And I propose the BBV method so you can calculate and track your BBV.

The first step is to select regional financial institutions with a similar size, in the below case $1 billion - $10 billion in total assets. I selected a bank in this group, First Bank of Nashville, Tennessee, because I was recently there. I then searched for banks with a similar loan composition to First Bank; fifty-to sixty percent commercial and commercial real estate loans to total loans. I netted yield on loans by their npa's/loans so those banks with riskier loan books are discounted. Banks that achieve a better than median yield on loans after netting npa's/loans, with a similar loan book in a similar region, likely do so because they are perceived to deliver better value to customers. i.e. brand. And First Bank passes this test, achieving 78 basis points over the loan peer median.

I then ran a second peer group for cost of interest bearing deposits. I kept it regional, and the same asset size range. And used less than 30% funded with time deposits, as First Bank was funded 27% with CDs. I could not use transaction accounts because of financial institutions' reclassing transaction accounts to savings/ money market accounts to reduce their Fed requirement.

Anything under the median cost of interest bearing deposits, I attributed to brand. This didn't work out so well for First Bank, as their cost of interest bearing deposits was 37 basis points greater than deposit peer median.

And then I added those two numbers together, giving a pre-tax brand value, and then tax effecting it and calculate as a percent of net income. If the bank is publicly traded, as First Bank is (Ticker: FBK), you can then calculate the BBV percent of net income as the percent of market capitalization to get an aggregate brand value. If not a publicly traded bank, you can calculate the BBV contribution to net income and multiply by a peer p/e multiple to get your aggregate BBV.

My suggestion is that you trend your BBV, looking to continuously improve. In First Bank's case, I would look to maintain my loan BBV advantage, and continuously improve my deposit one.

Imagine continuous improvement of BBV as a strategic planning SMART goal?

See the table. Calculate your own BBV. How did you fare?

1	Institution	First Bank
2	Parent	FB Financial Corporation
3	Ticker	FBK
4	Total Assets ($000)	5,133,339
5	Market Capitalization (4/7/19) ($MM)	1,044.9
6	Yield on Loans - (NPAs/Assets)	5.51%
7	Yield on Loans - (NPAs/Assets) Over Median	0.78%
8	Tax Effected Percent of Net Income	25%
9	Cost of Interest Bearing Liabilities	0.99%
10	Cost of Int. Brng Liabilities Under Median	-0.37%
11	Tax Effected Percent of Net Income	-14%
12	Brand Value as % of Market Cap (8+11)	11%
13	First Bank Aggregate Bank Brand Value ($MM)	118.0

~ Jeff

∞

It's worth emphasizing that when you gauge your brand value, you should do it over a trend line rather than a single point in time. And when selecting your loan peers, get as close as you can to your institution's loan mix and region. The same goes for selecting deposit peers, which will likely be different from the loan peers. Have at least five to 10 financial institutions to get a good average, and be prepared to drop institutions off the list when they merge or no longer have a similar loan or deposit mix. Other than that, remain consistent in your peers to reliably calculate whether you are increasing or decreasing your BBV over time.

In addition to Forbes, with its 8 percent ROE threshold for determining brand value, there are other sources that contend that anything over book value should be attributed to brand. For a couple of reasons, however, this approach doesn't work well with financial institutions.

For one thing, financial institutions vary in the relative amount of capital they carry on their balance sheets. The bank that keeps 10 percent capital will typically have a price-to-book trading multiple that is lower than the bank that has 8 percent capital, all other things being equal. But that doesn't mean the lower capitalized financial institution has greater brand value.

Second, financial institutions' valuations change significantly with changes in interest rates and the economy, because they are very sensitive to these macroeconomic factors. During the 2008 financial crisis and the 2020 pandemic, banks traded for significant periods of time below book value. But that doesn't mean their brand value eroded.

Shortly after publishing the first BBV article, I followed up with a second one—and it also landed among the top 20 most-read. The subject was the well-publicized case of a particular financial institution that had sold for no market price premium. It turned out to be a good exercise in putting the BBV calculation to the test. The theory was that the institution, although highly profitable, was widely regarded as one that grew its balance sheet based on price-driven volume and a super cheap infrastructure. Here is what I wrote.

∞

Why Did Oritani Sell for No Premium?

July 23, 2019

https://www.jeff4banks.com/2019/07/why-did-oritani-sell-for-no-premium.html

On June 25th, Oritani Financial Corp (ORIT) common stock closed at $16.21 per share. The next day they announced they were selling to Valley National Corp. for $16.29 per share. Virtually no premium. And less than ORIT traded one year ago. Why?

I was not part of the discussions regarding the transaction, and am not an advisor to either bank. I have no inside information to share. Only some observations and opinions.

ORIT has historically been a high performing financial institution in a highly concentrated deposit market. For the calendar first quarter 2019 they had a 1.22% ROA, which was down from 1.31% in fiscal 2018 (ORIT is on a different fiscal year). Their efficiency ratio... fuggetaboutit! Thirty six percent for the quarter ended 3/31.

So why did they receive 138% of book value, and 14x earnings when nearby (5 miles between headquarters) Stewardship Financial Corp. (SSFN) announced their sale to Columbia Financial (MHC) for 167% of book value, 17x earnings, and a whopping 77% premium. This transaction was also announced in June. ORIT is 4x the asset size of SSFN.

There are many factors that go into pricing merger transactions. Cost savings opportunities, attractiveness of markets, niches or specialties, seller's capitalization, buyers' stock valuations, etc. And in fact, ORIT was relatively highly capitalized compared to SSFN, with a leverage ratio of 12.92% versus 9.48%. That plays a role in price/book merger pricing. But ORIT consistently outperformed SSFN in financial performance. Yet received a lower valuation.

Bank Brand Value

You may recall I wrote about the value of brand in a post entitled: Bank Brand Value: Calculated! And I am very familiar with financial institutions in the Mid-Atlantic. So I suspected a key factor leading to the no-premium deal between ORIT and Valley might be related to ORIT's brand value.

So I did the calculation described in the above article (see table).

1	Institution	Oritani Bank
2	Parent	Oritani Financial Corp.
3	Ticker	ORIT
4	Total Assets ($000)	4,073,895
5	Market Capitalization (7/22/19) ($MM)	760.0
6	Yield on Loans - (NPAs/Assets)	3.87%
7	Yield on Loans - (NPAs/Assets) Over Median	-0.07%
8	Tax Effected Percent of Net Income	-4%
9	Cost of Interest Bearing Liabilities	1.38%
10	Cost of Int. Brng Liabilities Under Median	0.00%
11	Tax Effected Percent of Net Income	0%
12	Brand Value as % of Market Cap (8+11)	-4%
13	ORIT Aggregate Bank Brand Value ($MM)	(28.4)

I searched for regional peers with total assets between $1 billion and $10 billion. I then filtered for loan peers that had multi-family and commercial real estate loans greater than 60%. ORIT's was 92%. These are highly competitive, transactional loans. And in the New York metropolitan area, are significantly originated by loan brokers and bid on by banks.

Even though I searched for peers with high levels of these types of loans, ORIT earned seven basis points less than peer in Yield on Loans minus NPAs/Assets, negatively impacting bank brand value (BBV).

For deposits, I searched in the same region and size as loan peers, but controlled for banks that had total time deposits as a percent of deposits greater than 30%. ORIT's was 42%. The Cost of Interest Bearing Liabilities was the same as the deposit peer group. So it did not add or subtract from BBV.

So, although I filtered for financial institutions with a similar balance sheet composition, ORIT had an inferior Yield on Loans minus NPAs/Assets, and equivalent Cost of Interest Bearing Liabilities.

Leading me to the opinion that, among other factors, ORIT received no premium because it had a negative BBV.

Why do you think the bank received no premium?

~ Jeff

∞

I doubt Oritani put much weight behind the value of its brand. It did not appear to be part of its strategy. Cost advantage is a viable alternative to differentiation. And Oritani pursued it with zeal. The excess profits it amassed year over year may very well have been greater than any premium it might have received in a sale as a result of pursuing a presumably more expensive differentiation strategy. A bird in the hand is worth two in the bush. If Oritani management did the math and made a successful strategic decision on how to hit their goals, good for them.

In my experience, though, during strategy sessions, very few financial institutions claim to link their competitive advantage to cost advantage. That's been the case even when they exhibit behaviors in strategy execution that could be considered consistent with a cost-advantage approach. Such behaviors might include maintaining superior efficiency ratios or expense ratios to their peers, and pricing loans and deposits as if they have little brand value. In this sense, at least Oritani had alignment between what was likely its strategy and its behavior in its markets. In addition to that best-of-class efficiency ratio cited in the article, Oritani's expense ratio (non-interest expense to average assets) was 1.01 percent. Asset size was just over $4 billion when it sold. Needing more scale to achieve a cost advantage didn't seem necessary for this bank.

For other community financial institutions, however, the cost advantage strategy is either not desirable or not realistic. For them, the differentiation strategy makes more sense. And if that is your strategy, then your brand is critical to success. I can't imagine claiming the throne of brand leadership when a bank loosens covenants and lowers rates to get loan deals done and runs pricing specials to bring in deposits.

When it comes to premium branding, you know it when you see it. Take Mac users versus PC users. Mac has clearly created a brand that evokes loyalty, even at higher price points. How about Marriott customers? Even now that Marriott offers more than 32 distinct sub-brands with various price points, its loyalty program casts a Ritz-Carlton halo over its more accessible properties. And remember the old axiom, "you will never be fired for hiring IBM"? It still amazes me that many community financial institutions are willing to hire a big-three audit firm and pay two to three times the price of a regional firm.

Branding is not alchemy. The key is, you can manage what you can measure. And a superior brand should equate to some combination of three elements:

1) Charging more than competitors.
2) Keeping customers longer than competitors.
3) Getting more customers faster than competitors.

You can measure the first element by calculating your BBV, as described above. But what about the second and third elements?

Brand Equity and Customer Loyalty

Whether or not your customers will stick with you comes down to your brand equity. Brand equity is different from brand value in that, instead of calculating a financial return on brand, we are determining how customers feel about interacting with the brand. Of course, feelings are inherently more difficult to track than price premiums. But not impossible.

Northwestern University marketing professor and widely recognized branding expert Philip Kotler said brand equity can be tracked by averaging and weighting a set of metrics over time.[xxx] He suggests a blended mix of customer/prospect awareness, favorability level, and momentum. I would consider adding a fourth metric to that mix: customer longevity/loyalty.

At a financial institution, awareness and favorability would likely be measured by performing periodic and disciplined surveys. Baseline them and track them over time. Are you improving? Momentum may be more difficult. I would suggest two possible measures: deposit market share growth over time and increases or decreases in customer acquisition over time.

Customer longevity/loyalty should be measurable through a financial institution's internal systems. For example, what is the average duration of your financial institution's business checking account customers? This has financial as well as branding impacts, because the longer the duration of this product, the greater the credit given on deposit balances, and therefore the greater the spread and profitability.

For the community financial institution, brand equity is just as critical as brand value—if not more so—because it measures progress among customers and prospects alike. And if we look at the market share of the financial institutions, challenger banks, and fintechs that compete in our markets, we will realize that most businesses and households in our targeted geographies are prospects, not customers.

As Bruce Clapp, president of MarketMatch, a marketing and branding firm for community financial institutions, once said: "A brand is a collection of both perceptions and experiences. For non-customers, it is only built on perceptions, as they have no experience." How well do prospects know us? What do they think about us? And how much do they hear about us that will give our financial institution a shot at turning them into customers? If you see consistent improvement in those areas, your brand equity should go up.

And that brings us to the third element of a superior brand: getting customers faster than competitors.

Brand Equity and Turning Prospects into Customers

Any company in nearly any industry has limited resources it can dedicate to investments that don't have a clear payoff. Branding is typically one of the investments that's met with skepticism. Imagine a bank asking itself: "Should we bulk up the branding budget or invest in a new loan operating system?" You know the likely answer. That's why building a brand takes focused effort, disciplined tracking, and accountability.

I speak often of the concept of "sniper management." In a world of limited resources, we have to identify where the greatest opportunities exist—given our markets, capabilities, and technology—and concentrate efforts there. But when I ask financial institutions to single out their most profitable clients, create a profile of those clients, and identify the greatest opportunities to find more customers like them, I don't get data. I just hear anecdotes.

There's no reason for this to be the case. It is within the institution's control to measure the profitability of its lines of business, products, and customers. It's also true, however, that a point-in-time profit picture would not be adequate to identify the profile of the customers who should become the basis for differentiated experience at the institution.

Consider, for example, an early saver who opens a savings account with a small balance. Perhaps this saver graduated from college, and doesn't have much money yet, but does have a degree that indicates high earnings potential. The initial profitability of the customer would be low. And myopically focusing on point-in-time profitability won't put this customer—or similarly profiled customers—on your focus list for branding efforts.

This is why you need to take a lifetime-value approach. That low-balance savings account might exist for the first few years after college and yield a present-value customer profit of "x." The danger is that, as the customer migrates to higher-level savings, they'll drop off your radar. During these interim saving years—before they've reached an asset size appropriate for your wealth management group—they turn to a discount broker or robo-advisor. At this stage, the customer still yields low profits for the bank.

But then they buy a home, and then a larger home. Then they start a professional practice firm that needs a small cash flow loan, then a bigger loan to buy a building, then full cash management services. Now the profit picture looks different. That profile customer—although unprofitable initially—has the potential to deliver outsized lifetime value to your institution. If everyone took a short-time, spot-profitability approach to identifying key customer segments, we'd all end up pursuing large commercial real estate owners and investors.

The job of the financial institution is to find these key customers with high lifetime values and build a brand around what those customers want from a bank. Who are your doppelganger customers, based on the opportunities within your markets, the strengths of your financial institution, and the lifetime value of that customer segment? This level of sniper management will increase the likelihood that your brand resonates with customers and prospects. Because you are focused on who they are and what they need.

Brand and Your Other Stakeholders

For many financial institutions, shareholders are a key constituency. If you have shareholders, there are two sub-sets: existing shareholders and potential shareholders. Should you brand-build to them? Many community financial institutions don't. Or they put minimal effort into it by putting together slide decks and going to institutional investor dog-and-pony shows.

Branding aimed at shareholders, both existing and future, can deliver significant value. Take the case of JPMorgan Chase and Citigroup. Both have had mediocre financial performance recently, yet JPM trades at 160 percent price to tangible book value and 13x earnings per share, while Citi trades at 60 percent price to tangible book and 8x EPS. Why? I'm confident the iconic JPMorgan name (i.e. brand), with its rock-star CEO Jamie Dimon (i.e. his brand), and consistent financial performance leading to high investor and would-be investor credibility played a role.

How were these institutions positioned to shareholders? Demand for a financial institution's stock requires an active investor relations program to highlight the successes of the bank, the strength of its management team, and the attractiveness of the bank's markets. The company's brand can add significant value and play a key role in your institution being awarded higher market valuations than your peers. There are, of course, regulatory limitations on touting stock. But that doesn't mean a financial institution should punt on highlighting the credibility of the management team and consistency of company performance. Investors should feel good about holding your stock, and would-be investors should be aware of your company.

Employees are another significant constituency for brand building. Perhaps they're the most important one, because it is employees who deliver the brand message to customers, prospects, shareholders, communities, and other employees. The way employees feel about your institution helps you keep the keepers and attract future keepers. One simple way to measure how your brand resonates with employees is to measure tenure for all the employees you want to keep.

To Sum It Up…

This chapter suggests ways to calculate brand value and brand equity. What it does not do is prescribe how to *build* brand value and equity. I am skeptical that there are universal answers on how to achieve what we set out to calculate here. Likely, management's knowledge and experience, accompanied by experimentation and organizational learning, will yield a consistently better brand. In order to continually improve, you will need the operational discipline to track those elements that should result from a superior brand. And you'll need to make course corrections based on what you've learned. Remember: brand is not the sole responsibility of the marketing department. It is the responsibility of all.

Points Made This Chapter

❖ Brand is the connection of companies to their stakeholders.

❖ A superior brand should equate to some combination of: 1) charging more than competitors, 2) keeping customers longer than competitors, and/or 3) getting more customers faster than competitors.

❖ To assess whether you can charge more than competitors, calculate your bank brand value (BBV), as described above, and track its trend.

❖ Brand equity is determined by how customers feel about interacting with the brand.

❖ Brand equity can be calculated using customer/prospect awareness, favorability level, and momentum.

❖ In a world of limited resources, identify where the greatest opportunities exist—given our markets, capabilities, and technology—and concentrate branding efforts there.

❖ Don't limit building your brand to customers and prospects. Focus also on your employees, shareholders, and communities.

Chapter 10

The Hot Rate Stalemate

D o you shop at Whole Foods or Aldi? Why? It would be instructive to compare a premium brand that has earned your loyalty to an unbranded version of the same product or service. Make two columns, and in rows write reasons why you prefer the premium brand over the generic. And, by the same token, take note of why you believe someone would pick the generic brand.

Now do the same with your financial institution and one or more market share leaders in your geography. Be brutally honest. Who are your most coveted customers, and why should they pick you over the competition? Do they pick you? I'm not asking for an anecdote from last month when a happy customer approached you in the parking lot. This exercise calls for measurable data.

Don't let hubris cloud your self-assessment. In the FDIC's most recent Summary of Deposits, all of the top five U.S. financial institutions grew deposits. Two of them grew deposit market share despite being unable to acquire other banks, as they already had more than 10 percent market share of deposits nationwide. The third largest depository, Wells Fargo, went from 11.43 percent to 10.76 percent market share while they were under a consent order that limited their growth. And yet, they still grew deposits by $184 billion during the year.

We make premium pricing decisions every day. For reasons that may differ by customer, we place a greater monetary value on a branded good or service than its generic version. We do so even when it is difficult to justify paying the higher price. I bought a cup of coffee at a Starbucks at a turnpike rest stop. There was a Burger King next to it, and I checked their coffee price. I paid 32 percent more just to have Starbucks on my cup. Does Starbucks serve better coffee? Depends who—and how—you ask. The more important question is how customers feel drinking Starbucks versus Burger King coffee.

Apicius, a first century Roman, purportedly came up with the aphorism: "We eat first with our eyes."[xxxi] A while back I heard a brand expert expand on this concept, claiming we "think with our eyes." Her story was about a well-healed restaurant that served a $13 cup of coffee. Except one night they served instant coffee. And people thought it was terrific. She opined it was because it was served in an elegant restaurant, with well-appointed décor, a polished wait staff, and classical background music. It wasn't taste that drove customers to believe they were having a great cup of coffee.

Can bankers create an environment where customers believe they are getting a terrific cup of coffee? I think so—yet so many are challenged by it. So they choose to compete on rates. Here is what I wrote about using rate to lure customers. It might hit close to home and hurt a bit.

∞

Hot Rates – Swipe Left

May 10, 2018

https://www.jeff4banks.com/2018/05/hot-rates-swipe-left.html

Retail customers are not growing at community financial institutions.

According to my firm's profitability outsourcing service, branches have fewer retail checking accounts than two years ago. Deposit gains were made through growth in average balances per account.

If you're a commercial bank, you may be fine if this trend is happening at your institution. So I ask you, what percent of your deposits are retail?

You should check. Because even the most commercial of commercial banks tend to have significant retail deposits. And if you are losing retail customers, how do you win them back?

Loan to deposit ratios have been on the rise over the past couple of years (see chart). Regulators are starting to ask a lot more questions about your liquidity during exams. Our ALCO meetings have done an about face from the 2012 "what are we going to do with all of this money?" to "how are we going to fund next month's loan pipeline?"

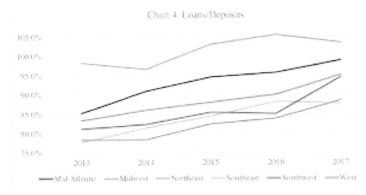

Chart 4: Loans/Deposits

And when you ask about funding next month, you rely on short-term, tactical fixes. We're not talking strategy here.

In comes the rate promotion. It's like 2006 all over again.

And it's too bad. Because so many readers of these pages have done an excellent job "righting" their deposit mix to be less dependent on hot money. And we have had plenty of time to anticipate funding pinches, given the three year trend of loans growing faster than deposits.

When I asked a community bank director of marketing about rate promotions and the success at turning them into loyal, core deposit customers, she was skeptical. The very premise of how you got that customer should tell you that they value rate above all else. And what is different today than 2006 is how easy it is to move money between financial institutions, and how transparent the rate environment is. A quick search on "bank rate promotions" gave me a trove of sites to compare offers.

It is difficult enough to turn retail customers into profitable customers. Balances and spreads drive revenues. Winning a $100,000 account isn't much of a win if you can only drive five basis points of spread from it. Better to get a $10,000 account at a 300 basis point spread, right (math)? But to fund the pipeline, I would need ten of those accounts. That is why core deposit gathering is so strategic.

If you are struggling to fund loans, it may not be too late to avoid the 2%, 13-month CD promo.

Here are some suggestions:

1. **Reward existing core deposit customers** - In a recent conversation with a bank marketer, they spoke of the power of word of mouth marketing among one of their customer niches. Imagine the word of mouth marketing if you shared your institution's financial success with core depositors in the form of a special dividend to them. Execution is key. Use a long-term average balance as your guide, encouraging loyalty, and keeping more of their deposits at your bank. Better than paying non-depositors, right?

2. **Flash sale to core depositors** - Along the same theme, reward your core deposit customers with a "flash sale" rate promotion to gain more of their deposit dollars. Execute wisely. Do those customers have a "real" core deposit account with you, that has direct deposit going into it, and the electric bill coming out of it? Don't fear mass promoting it, as non-customers may get the feeling "hey, I want to be a customer there".

3. **Build relationships** - I hear this a lot among bankers, but don't see it a lot. As I have said on so many occasions, I have not been called by my current bank. Ever. And I think my experience is not unique. I know nobody there. But if I have a relationship with a banker, and the bank does not conspire to

"screw" me (see below), then I would be open to bringing more balances to them.

4. **Don't screw your customers** – I wrote about this in the article "A Time of Reckoning for Your Bank's Core Deposits?"[xxxii] Having products match market interest rates automatically is an ALCO nightmare. But paying 1/3 the market rates on a customers' savings, and then bragging about it in your investor presentations, can't be a way to strengthen relationships and increase the amount of business you do with them. Could this be a reason why customers spread out their banking relationships?

If you are reading this, and you are having some liquidity pinches, it might be too late to execute on the above and get funding for next month's loan pipeline. And perhaps some wholesale approaches would work to relieve the pressure.

But, long-term, don't give up the core funding gains you worked so hard to achieve.

What do you suggest to get more short-term retail funding into your bank?

~ Jeff

∞

Too often, I hear bankers and consultants discuss balance sheet management techniques that amount to taking advantage of customers who aren't paying attention to what their "trusted advisor" is doing. I put trusted advisor in quotes because that's the term used in strategy sessions. No one ever says, "Let's take advantage of our customers." Is your institution's strategy to be trusted by customers? If so, then running a seven-month CD special with the idea that at maturity, 70 percent of takers will roll their CDs into the lower, six-month rate is inconsistent. It certainly doesn't create strategic alignment.

Rates and yields are nebulous terms to customers. Price and cost are better understood, but not really used in banking. The cost of a Starbucks coffee is more straightforward than the "cost" of your money market account.

Terminology issues aside, there are customers who focus on price. The rate shoppers. And if your financial institution is pursuing a competitive advantage through cost rather than differentiation, perhaps the "hot rate" approach to acquiring customers is aligned with your strategy.

But for those banks pursuing a differentiation strategy, it's important to break the "hot rate" addiction. Price is the quickest way to get growth. Yet pursuing a Ritz-Carlton differentiation strategy at Holiday Inn pricing makes little sense. On paper, few would admit to taking that approach. Yet at times, some look like they are doing it in practice.

Can we differentiate in such a way that customers don't demand the best rates? Here are some ideas.

Store of Value versus Accumulation Accounts

Consider dividing your accounts into two categories: store of value and accumulation. As far as the customer is concerned, deposits that facilitate transactions or short-term saving are store of value assets. In other words, those customers are likely to be less concerned about rate as they are about safety, access, efficient transaction processing, and stable value… i.e., a store of value. Such accounts would include the traditional checking account and savings for next year's vacation or an upcoming vehicle purchase. It would be a mistake to think of these customers as rate sensitive and behave as if they were. The priority for these accounts should be a frictionless customer experience.

But that same customer might also have an emergency fund, college savings, and a portion of retirement savings at your bank. They want these accounts to grow—at least enough to keep pace with inflation. For accumulation accounts like these, customers may be rate sensitive. They might not demand the top rate. But they'll expect a competitive rate. I know of no research on price points that test the loyalty of a long-term customer. So aim for the point where the bank's advice, attentiveness, convenience, and quality of the banker/customer relationship are in equilibrium with the rate paid (or charged if for a loan).

Consider a depositor with a main checking account, two savings accounts, a money market account, and a couple of CDs. This would likely be an attractive customer. And the blended cost of funds of this relationship would likely be profitable to the financial institution. So why run a seven-month CD special to get more of their money—only to antagonize them by quietly dropping the rate when the CD matures? That is "hot rate" mentality, and it will strain the limits of your customer's loyalty.

Instead, manage the profitability of the customer to meet certain hurdle rates established by your institution. For example, you could look at pre-tax ROE, using allocated equity as the denominator—or ROA, using account balances as the denominator. If your institution lacks this management reporting, use cost of funds for the entire relationship as the guardrail. Empower relationship managers to balance pricing decisions so long as profits remain within certain parameters.

Stretch Your Thinking on Price Elasticity

If demand for your financial institution's services is highly sensitive to price, that means it's price elastic. If price doesn't much change the demand, it's inelastic. For financial services, however, it's more than likely that price elasticity of demand varies by customer. Common sense tells us that non-customers are more sensitive to price, because they don't currently bank with you. Existing customers are more inelastic. This phenomenon often leads bankers to offer non-customers higher deposit rates—or lower loan rates—to entice them to become customers. The profit gaps caused by incentive pricing for non-customers motivates bankers to make this up on the shoulders of existing customers.

This dilemma might very well be the reason why my "Hot Rates" article received so many views. It flips the perverse incentive to reward price-sensitive non-customers. Instead, banks should be providing incentives for existing customers to bring more of their business to us and remain with us longer. This approach aligns the bank with the success of its customers.

How can bankers determine each customer's price elasticity? As noted, if we aspire to deliver Ritz-Carlton service, we don't want to charge Holiday Inn prices. This implies some discount in deposit rates from no-brand banks, and some premium on loan rates. But what discount and what premium? Since each customer's sensitivity is somewhat different, an empowered banker, operating within previously determined profit hurdles and compliance guardrails, can make those decisions. It can be a key strength that differentiates the community financial institution from super-regional or national competitors that dominate most markets.

Make Your Brand Part of the Customer's Personal Brand

"My broker's EF Hutton, and Hutton says…"[xxxiii] This famous line was from a 1970s television advertisement created by ad agency Benton & Bowles. Aside from positioning EF Hutton as a premium brand, it projected that brand glow onto the customer. It made the customer feel important that he was associated with EF Hutton. Can financial institutions create a brand that burnishes the personal brand of customers—like when people brag, "I gotta have my Starbucks"? Such a brand, the logic goes, should result in greater price inelasticity and an increased pricing delta between your financial institution and a no-brand competitor.

True story: After a bank board of directors meeting a number of years ago, a director approached me on a different topic regarding something his Merrill Lynch broker told him. This was a bank that had a significant trust department—and yet one of its directors had his money at Merrill Lynch. Not only that, it felt like he wanted me to know he was a Merrill client. In the eyes of the director, Merrill Lynch elevated his brand. We see similar behavior playing out with cars, restaurants, clothing brands, and country clubs. People associate with brands that help build their personal brand. Can your financial institution be a part of your customers' and prospects' brand palette—one that allows you to price for the level of service you provide?

I think so. But if you've regularly used the hot rate gambit, it will take discipline to align your strategy, culture, and operating environment to become an institution that gets paid for the difference you deliver.

To Sum It Up...

If your financial institution's competitive advantage is cost leadership, then perhaps you use rate to attract customers. If your operating expense is, say, top quartile—or 30 basis points below peers—you can afford to pay 15 basis points more for deposits or charge 15 basis points less on loans. You would still be more profitable, all other things being equal. But if differentiation is your strategy, you must build the operational discipline to attract the customers who value whatever makes you different. You must empower bankers to price products to meet customer needs. And you must track progress on how you're getting paid for delivering Ritz-Carlton service.

Points Made This Chapter

❖ Why would customers pick you over the competition? No, seriously, you should find out.

❖ People make premium pricing decisions every day.

❖ Overall, community financial institutions are not growing their number of retail customers. Their deposit gains are attributable to growth in average deposits per account.

❖ Using rate promotions to grow your customer count may not yield the type of customer that is consistent with your strategy. The very premise of how you got that customer should tell you that they value rate above all else.

❖ If you use rate promotions, use them to reward existing core deposit customers and attract more of their business.

❖ Empower bankers to make pricing decisions, within boundaries.

❖ To increase loyalty without using price, build a brand where customers brag that they bank with you.

Chapter 11

Product < Product Management

Product management involves assessing demand for a product; coordinating processes and technology; designing, launching, and marketing the product; and continually seeking profit improvements throughout the product's life cycle. It's important work. So why are product managers so rare at financial institutions? Sure, some of the largest banks have them. But is that common among the majority? Not really.

Let's face it: bank products are never the shiniest object in the room. Yet product is the first pillar in the four p's of marketing: product, place, price and promotion. Are the four p's still relevant? Not according to John Oxford, chief marketing officer at Renasant Bank in Tupelo, Mississippi. In his 2020 book, *No More Next Time: Marketing in the Age of Distraction*, he introduces the four c's as the new pillars of bank marketing: content, connection, conversion, and campaigns.[xxxiv] In industries where products are barely distinguishable from competitor to competitor, he argues, creating a connection with target customers could be the differentiation that pushes that customer to choose you. The sales funnel, in this context, is much different from what it's been in the past. And financial institutions are better off focusing on getting target customers into the funnel, managing the sales process, and then into the relationship management process.

So the thinking goes. But does that mean product management in banking is dead? What is the purpose of a sales process that leads target customers to a product that isn't uniquely suited to them? What's the point of any sale if your financial institution can't deliver it profitably?

When speakers at conferences invoke terms that bear little resemblance to their audiences' everyday reality, it is worth noting. And it was at a conference a few years back that I heard the term "product" mentioned frequently enough to make me wonder. In my experience there, the audience had little sense of urgency around products and product management. Here is what I wrote about it.

∞

Bank Products: Blah Blah Blah

October 1, 2017

https://www.jeff4banks.com/2017/10/bank-products-blah-blah-blah.html

At a recent banking conference, Ray Davis of Umpqua Bank took center stage to tell of his journey from a small, Oregon community bank to a regional powerhouse. He mentioned products only briefly. And product was not part of the bank's success. I thought, Why?

Stuck on the topic, I jotted down the products that I remembered from when I landed my first banking job in 1985 while Davis spoke. I never claimed to have a great attention span. And I used those hotel notepads. Someone has to use them. Here was my list:

Products Circa 1985

Mortgage loan

Car loan

Personal loan

Home equity loan (?)

Business loan and line of credit

Commercial mortgage loan

Construction Loan

Checking account (business and personal)

Savings account (business and personal)

Certificate of deposit (business and personal)

Merchant services (?)

Trust

Then I wrote down how that list has changed.

New Products: Circa Today

Money market accounts (although could be classified as hyped savings)

Investments

Sweep accounts/cash management

Hedging

Options

The hedging and options might be categorized as features of business loans, versus products in and of themselves. But let's not quibble over insignificance.

What do you notice about the above lists?

What I notice is there is little difference in the products of today and the products when MacGyver developed improvised explosive devices with his shoes.

Bank products, at their base, have not changed. So, perhaps, instead of developing complexity in our product set, we should look to develop simplicity. Wouldn't we all benefit from more simplicity?

What sparked this post was a recent article in ababankmarketing.com written by Mark Gibson and Kevin Halsey of Capital Performance Group in Washington DC. It was a precursor to a presentation they gave at the ABA Marketing Conference in New Orleans titled "How to Build Remarkable Products".[xxxv] One of their slides from that presentation is below, courtesy of b2bmarketingexperiences.com.

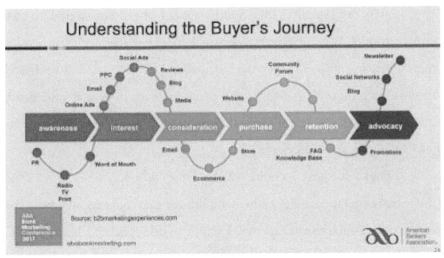

This slide, and another I was privileged to see, dubbed as one of the most popular by the authors, speaks nothing of product. In fact, I will confess to you that when I hear bankers talk about products, product management, product design, etc., I have no idea what they are talking about. Bank products have been the same since I've been in banking.

Yes, there are different features to products, such as high interest rates for checking account customers that engage in specific behaviors, or option-based CD's as developed by Neil Stanley of The CorePoint. Still a checking account. And still a CD.

Distribution is different. Back to my notepad, I penned the 1985 distro points as person-person, in-branch, telephone, and ATM. Today we could add online, mobile, and social (for customer service). As a list, not very impressive.

However, in terms of customer utilization, distribution has been massively disrupted.

Sure, bankers can tick off all of the new features added to that standard product list, as mentioned above. But new products? Hardly.

So why not simplify? Like Southwest did when they went with one airplane model. Why not have a personal checking account, that is non-interest bearing up to a certain average balance, which could differ based on customer utilization that could easily by solved by AI, and bears interest above that level. Same with business checking, now that we can pay interest on those accounts.

Savings accounts could easily have sub-accounts. Like the proverbial envelopes in the night stand drawer that tucks money away for certain things such as Emergency, Vacation, and Holiday. I believe PNC did this with the Virtual Wallet account. To me, Virtual Wallet is nothing more than a practically thought out savings account.

I recently commented to a bank's strategy team that I thought the days when bankers could rely on sleepy money are coming to an end. The

13-month CD special trick, where the CD reprices at the lower 12-month CD when it matures, is over. A business model that relies on the stupidity of your customers will die. Imagine a customer getting a text from a financial management app that says "your bank is screwing you". It may not say that, but it would say that a CD is maturing and the rate it will roll into is below market.

No, we can no longer rely on sleepy money. But perhaps we should focus Marketing on touching the customer in every phase of the buying journey instead of concocting schemes to complicate products, tinker with pricing, and rely on Rip Van Winkle customers. This is what I believe my friends at Capital Performance Group were emphasizing.

If I were a marketer, I would focus on simplicity in product design. And sophistication in the customer acquisition or relationship expansion funnel.

But I'm not a marketer.

~ Jeff

∞

Simple yet functional products. What might that look like? The neo-bank Chime separates accounts into two categories: spending and saving. Sound like a checking account and savings account to you? These simple accounts are ornamented with useful features, such as "round up" automatic savings, in which Chime simply moves money from the

spending to the savings account. There are automatic alerts, "cover me" overdraft protection, and "spot me" payday lending. Delivered with an elegant mobile app.

They do nothing groundbreaking. Do you have checking and savings products? Can you send customers automatic alerts based on activity? Can you set the customer up to automatically move money between "spending" and savings accounts? My guess is you can. They simply do it well. The difference between them and you is that they don't have branches—and the associated expenses—so therefore they can pay higher rates. But they also don't have personnel to sit side by side with customers, to set all of this up based on customers' individual goals and dreams. You, however, likely do. But to make the effort profitable, you have pay attention and be ready to make adjustments throughout the product's life cycle.

Product Management Culture

When banks talk about product management, they often mean that a business case is made, projections conjured, a campaign developed, the product is operationalized, and compliance procedures are put in place. Next, the bank launches its campaign, and starts booking new customers and accounts. Then what? Without the support of a product management culture, it will be tough for all that effort to reach its potential.

That's because product management doesn't start with a needs assessment and end with a successful campaign. You've developed projections. Now you must track whether the product is meeting your targets. Profits are the measuring stick for success. Was the product properly designed and in sufficient demand to generate volume so the cost per account goes down? Is it priced right, so that the combined fees and spread meet your profit hurdles? Based on your results, you must implement improvements to make it profitable—and then continue to manage the product through its entire life cycle.

Unfortunately, banks are challenged to report product profitability in a useful manner. It's not for lack of tools. Most core processors and many fintechs offer the software platforms. And if you lack the expertise, you can always turn to outsourcing firms for help—just as many community banks outsource ALCO reporting. But many bankers must think they don't need product profitability reporting. I say they do. When a financial institution understands the profit drivers, and is committed to continuous improvement, it develops the operating discipline to assess, implement, improve, and ultimately retire products. In other words, it cultivates a product management culture.

Product Profitability Levers

In a product management culture, the owner of the product monitors revenue. Here's an example of what that might look like:

For traditional spread products, like a "sole proprietor checking" account, the biggest source of revenue is the spread generated by the average balance in each account. And spread is calculated by the rate paid. For sole proprietor checking, that would likely be zero, offset by a notional "credit for funds" (CFF), which is the rate charged by a lender to the bank, such as a Federal Home Loan Bank borrowing of the same duration.

So if the CFF for the sole proprietor checking is 2 percent—and the average balance in the account is $40,000—then the spread revenue per year would be $800. If the bank is in a rising interest rate environment, that spread is likely to grow. That is why money center banks ramp up their checking campaigns in a growing economy and rising rate environment. The profitability of core deposit products (and therefore branches) grows. Remember receiving offers of $400 to move your checking account? Where are those campaigns when the Fed Funds Rate is zero? Money center banks know their numbers when developing that offer.

On the other hand, if interest rates are declining, spread—and therefore profitability—is likely to shrink. If the spread isn't enough to generate the desired profit that was anticipated during product design, there are levers the product manager can pull:

Stickiness – The CFF for non-term deposits like checking accounts is based on the duration of the product. To boost the CFF, the product manager could introduce features—like positive pay or automatic messaging—that increase the stickiness of the customer and balances. As a result, the extended duration could stretch the CFF from 2 percent to 2.5 percent. That would increase revenues, and therefore profits, so long as the spread increase exceeds any operating expense increases because of the added features.

Average balance – The product manager could also analyze the industry codes for sole proprietor checking accounts to determine those professions that tend to carry higher balances. What if, say, veterinarians carry $50,000 average balances? Those accounts would generate $1,000 per account per year, $200 more than the overall average. As the bank targets more of the higher-balance customer cohorts, the average balance of the product—and therefore its profitability—creeps northward.

Fee structure – If increasing the spread proves challenging, it might be an opportunity to look at the fee structure. Is the bank collecting what it has projected in fees? If not, why not? Perhaps the fee structure is appropriate, but the waived fees are much higher than anticipated. More discipline might be warranted to increase fee income and overall profitability of the product. That conversation starts with the product manager communicating with the line-of-business manager, who has fee waiving authority.

Cost – Determining the cost of a product can be challenging, because banks are not typically organized by product. A sole proprietor checking account will draw its costs from most areas of the bank. However, if the assumptions used to determine the cost per account are consistently applied, then the cost should be directionally correct. And bank cost structures are mostly fixed. Compensation is the greatest expense at almost every financial institution, and in my observation, it is nearly 90 percent fixed. Technology—though there may be some per-account costs—is largely fixed and tied to a contract. Occupancy expense cares nothing about how much or little product volume you drive through the building. It's fixed except for slight variations in utilities expense.

In this highly fixed cost environment, product volume is like a magic wand that lowers cost per account. Product managers who are not satisfied with their product's profitability, yet are challenged to increase revenues, can decrease costs simply by selling more product. At its fundamental level, this is how a financial institution achieves economies of scale—by lowering cost per account as the product portfolio grows. As the product becomes more profitable, so does the bank.

If lowering cost by increasing volume does not yield the desired result, the product manager could look for process improvements. The idea here is to decrease the resources needed to originate and maintain the product. Sole proprietor checking, for example, likely uses wire transfer resources. Perhaps the bank could switch to a wire transfer system with the ability to verify transactions without bank employee intervention. That could free up resources to handle significantly more wires, reducing the wire transfer department's cost allocation per account. The cost goes down.

Hurdle rates – Most disciplined product management functions have ROE hurdle rates as their target. This presumes an equity allocation based on the bank's perceived risk of the product. Sole proprietor checking, while having very little credit risk, still faces interest rate and liquidity risks, among others. The bank risk officer or committee may deem a 1 percent equity allocation appropriate. And the ROE hurdle might be 20 percent.

One percent on the $40,000 sole proprietor checking is $400. Twenty percent of $400 is $80. If each account had, on average, $800 in annual spread revenue, $100 in actual fees, minus an operating cost per account of $600, it exceeds its ROE hurdle ($300 profit when the hurdle was $80). Manage the trend, make course corrections, and grow profits.

Pulling the plug – A bank with a high level of operating discipline requires a product manager who is responsible for the continual profit improvement of the product. Each product should strike the balance between demand—which drives pricing and volumes—and costs, so that as it matures, the product achieves economies of scale and desired profits. But the financial institution should also have the information needed to assess what stage of the life cycle each product is in. And it should be ready pull the plug on the products in decline. If you don't waste resources on dying products, you can invest in what is in demand.

Product Personalization

The days of creating stagnant products for a wide swath of customer cohorts is dying. Silver Haired Checking, you ask? Designing a near-fixed feature checking product to entice retirees is not the personalized customer experience that Amazon is currently delivering to its shoppers. When you go to Amazon, it recommends products specific to you, based on your buying and search patterns, consistent with your demographic. It doesn't offer every retiree the same bucket of products.

Technology allows us to do this. We can now create a menu of optional features on our accounts. It's like when we stand at the car rental checkout desk and they offer us enhanced insurance, gas fill up, a GPS, and a baby seat. But banks can do it in such a way that doesn't annoy the customer, like we might get annoyed at the car rental desk.

With a menu of options, there could be hundreds of unique account types that carry certain features. Of course, this might drive a backwards-looking operations department crazy. On the other hand, it could improve competitiveness, volumes, and technology utilization for the forward-looking bank. And given societal propensity to pay for subscriptions, if priced right, it could enhance fee income and therefore product profitability.

Imagine having a base small business checking account that offers 20 optional features. The customer could select the desired features on account opening—or afterwards if they later determine they need it. In a pre-packaged account design world, the customer would get all 20 features, willy-nilly. And because the customer did not "opt-in" for any of those features, it becomes more difficult to collect fees on them to offset the increased costs. Sort of like getting C-SPAN in your cable lineup.

With highly personalized options, the customer might choose positive pay for $1 per month, and identity theft protection for $2 per month, but not select the "lower-my-bills" analysis tool or the free-ATM-anywhere option. The customer designed their own account and volunteered to pay $3 per month for the features *they* selected.

This will be table stakes for financial institutions in the future. With it, product managers will benefit from many more levers and price points they can tweak to increase the profit trend of products. And that will ultimately lead to a more profitable bank with greater resources to serve all stakeholders.

To Sum It Up…

Banking products haven't changed materially in the past 35 years. So why do we think there is some new product out there that might rocket our financial institution to the top of the innovation spectrum? Would it be better to do what Southwest Airlines does? That is, create a simple product suite and deliver it in such a distinctive, frictionless way that we distinguish ourselves from the competition. As Amazon's founder Jeff Bezos once said, "Our customers are not responsible for our profitability." True—but someone is.

If a financial institution establishes a product management discipline, then products can go through their life cycles and evolve. Course corrections can be made to balance the demands of customers with the bank's bottom line. Thus, you can operationalize your own innovation.

Points made this chapter:

❖ Product management is not a common core discipline in financial institutions.

❖ The four p's of marketing are being replaced with the four c's: content, connection, conversion, campaign. But that shouldn't stop the product manager from using price to strike the balance between cost and demand.

❖ Bank products haven't changed much in 35 years. Distribution and delivery have. But not products.

❖ Product management doesn't start with a needs assessment and end with a successful campaign. It runs through the entire product life cycle.

❖ Product management is key in determining where exactly a product is in its life cycle.

❖ Product personalization is becoming table stakes for financial institutions.

Chapter 12

What to Do About Consumer Lending

You've seen the law of unintended consequences in action. When bad actors infiltrate a market and stick it to the consumer, the government takes note and often steps in. It passes laws. It ramps up regulation. It roots out as many bad actors as possible. In the process, it steamrolls over anything in its way. And in the case of consumer lending, "in its way" has been the vast majority of financial institutions that made fairly-priced consumer loans to those who needed them.

Federal laws applicable to consumer and residential lending include: Truth in Lending Act (TILA) (Reg Z), Equal Credit Opportunity Act (Reg B), Real Estate Settlement Procedures Act (RESPA), Fair Credit Reporting Act (Reg V), Home Mortgage Disclosure Act, Military Lending Act, Servicemembers Civil Relief Act, and the Fair Debt Collection Practices Act. That last one regulates third party debt collectors. But since many financial institutions employ these providers, the cost gets passed through the banking system. This list does not include state laws, which surely add another layer of complexity for the average bank.

In many instances, the consumer does need protection from the devious behaviors of bad actors. The challenge, however, is navigating the elevated cost and the legal risk to the good actors—i.e., the thousands of community financial institutions that get caught up in the maelstrom. The median cost to originate and maintain a home equity loan or line of credit (HELOC) is approximately $1,300, according to The Kafafian Group, the community financial institution consultancy where I work. An unsecured personal loan costs the bank $600. The lowest cost consumer loan is an indirect vehicle loan, at just shy of $200. That figure is so low because the financial institution doesn't own the distribution costs. The auto dealer does. Telling.

TRID—the TILA/RESPA Integrated Disclosure rule, enforced by the Consumer Finance Protection Bureau—is such an expensive piece of regulation that it drove many community financial institutions out of fixed-term home equity lending. That's because those loans are subject to TRID compliance, whereas HELOCs are not. Some creative financial institutions have gotten around that by starting borrowers off with a HELOC and then allowing them to "fix" their first draw. After that, the loan behaves like a fixed-term home equity, but without the risk of muffing the TRID disclosure. How about that?

Such conditions have eroded or eliminated the profitability of consumer lending for all but the highest volume shops—those able to drive down such costs. As a result, few community financial institutions treat consumer lending as an integral part of their strategy. If they offer these loans at all, it's merely as an accommodation to customers. In its zeal to pursue bad actors, the government has been driving all but the largest players out of the market.

But consumer lending is part and parcel to what most believe a community bank should be. A local resource that offers credit to members of its community. And the inability to do so has caused considerable hand wringing among bank management teams and boards of directors. This is what likely drew people in such large numbers to my original article on the topic.

∞

Consumer Lending: Should Banks Do It?

April 12, 2018

https://www.jeff4banks.com/2018/04/consumer-lending-should-banks-do-it.html

We're running out of assets.

When I first read Standards Needed for Safe, Small Installment Loans from Banks, Credit Unions[xxxvi] by the Pew Charitable Trusts that encouraged financial institutions to get back into small ticket consumer lending, I thought "what are they nuts!"

Consumer loans for those banks that utilize my firm's outsourced profitability reporting service lost (0.26%) as a percent of the average consumer loan portfolio in the fourth quarter. And it wasn't an anomaly. Ever since we formed our company in 2001, this has been the case.

Sure, home equity lines of credit made 0.71% for the fourth quarter. But it was the only sub-product that showed a profit. Fixed home equity loans… nope. Indirect loans, unsecured personal loans? No and no. So why would banks expand small-ticket, unsecured personal lending?

Because we're running out of assets. Pretty soon we'll be left with small to mid-sized business loans and commercial real estate that isn't big enough for large banks or conduits. And there are FinTechs, loan brokers, insurance companies, and investment funds chipping away at them.

Mortgage lending is getting away from us. Mortgage bankers and brokers own a significant share of market (although less than prior to the 2007-08 financial crisis). And Quicken Loans is in the top 5 HMDA market share in nearly every market we analyze. Oh, and Quicken is hammering away at home equity lending too.

We lost auto loans to the indirect market. Who comes to our branch for a car loan today? If we don't consider how we intend to defend our small business and CRE lending, and re-enter some of these other loan markets, we may end up as a balance sheet for hire. Which we already do via buying mortgage back securities and using loan brokers in metro areas.

Are you ready to be Web Bank, part deux?

So I reconsidered my knee-jerk reaction to the Pew Charitable Trusts report. Most community financial institution strategies has some sort of "community" focus. It's implied whenever someone says "we're a community bank." Which nearly everyone does. Even the big banks. So maybe we should put some moxy behind those words. Profitable moxy, though. Not charitable moxy.

Why do consumer loans consistently lose money? Looking at our peer group numbers, the consumer loan costs a little above $1,100 per year in operating expense to originate and maintain. Expensive. This is a fully absorbed number. Meaning that all bank resources that are dedicated to the consumer loan function is fully allocated to the product, whether they are being used or not. And recently, they have not been used.

For example, there is a fair amount of branch expense in that number, because branches are typically responsible for originating those loans, and participate in their maintenance. If we got rid of consumer loans, that expense would migrate elsewhere. And if we are not originating new loans, then resources dedicated to origination, such as branch staff and credit, for example, are dormant but must be paid for by the existing loans in the portfolio.

Four Ways to Bring Back Consumer Loans, Drive Volume, and Increase Profits

1. **Make consumer loans more than an accommodation.** Not many financial institutions consider consumer loans as a strategically important product group that will drive growth and profitability into the future. Perhaps it is because of the hurdles to achieving meaningful growth and market share. Or the competitors that wedged themselves into the dominant market position. But if executive management and the Board aren't committed to pursuing consumer lending to be more prominent on your balance sheet, then you will not succeed.

2. **Align your credit culture and risk appetite to be successful consumer lenders.** It is not lost on me that the last bastion of consumer lending at banks is home equity loans. Real estate secured. Hard collateral. Relatively low charge-offs. It is difficult to change that mindset when doing loans with little to no collateral, such as small ticket consumer or credit cards. Charge-off rates of 4%-5% with no collateral? Yes. Get used to it (other than home equity). Or don't do it.

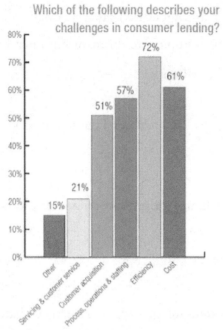

Which of the following describes your challenges in consumer lending?

3. Drive down costs. Regulation has driven up costs and made us gun shy. But we can't continue to put $1,100 of resources per year into a consumer loan. Especially if the loan balance is $2,500. How can we possibly make money on that? We can't. The ABA recently conducted a survey on the State of Digital Lending (see chart)[xxxvii] that said that, although consumers were happy with how smooth and quick online lending decisions were made, online lenders only received a 26% approval rating, versus 75% for banks. Driving more volume will drive down costs by putting under-utilized resources to work, and digitizing end-to-end will reduce the amount of resources needed for consumer lending.

4. **Price right.** Even if banks cut the cost of originating and maintaining consumer loans in half, to $550, what rate will they have to charge to make a reasonable profit? Let's say a reasonable profit is a 1.5% pre-tax profit as a percent of the portfolio. And the non-home equity portion experienced a

4.5% charge-off rate. And the cost of funds for such lending is 1%. If the average loan size was, say, $3,000, the bank would have to charge an effective yield of 25.3% (($550/3,000)+1%+4.5%+1.5%). Those rates get the scrutiny of do-gooders and "champions of the people" that could cause negative press. And keeps community financial institutions out of this business. Take note Pew Charitable Trusts. However, knowing this math, the bank can work at pressing the levers needed to do this lending profitably, at the right price, that benefits borrowers and the banks. And keeps those borrowers out of the hands of the sharks that prey on their misfortune.

Should we give up on consumer lending?

~ Jeff

∞

I still stand by those four recommendations. And I would add a fifth: Align technology and artificial intelligence with employee capabilities to differentiate your bank from competitors. Make your bank the one that's willing to advise customers. To let them know that borrowing against their house, an appreciating asset, to finance Christmas presents, depreciating assets, is a bad idea. To warn them that the car they are considering is too expensive for their budget. To help customers develop habits that result in spending less than they make. To help customers build wealth. Not when they already have wealth. But when they have nothing.

The Pew research report I cited in my article states that "80 percent of Americans think that a $60 charge for a $400, three-month loan is fair, though its APR is 88 percent." That amount, however, would still be far short of covering the costs for such a loan. It also doesn't cover the financial counseling that is likely needed to help borrowers emerge from a vicious cycle of cash shortfalls, expensive loans, struggles to pay back the loans, and so forth. Indeed, the same report says that payday lenders serve only 500 customers per storefront. There is plenty of repeat business. The need for better lending services is out there. The challenge is to do it at a profit—and without inviting intervention from critics who often don't understand the complexity of the problem or the unintended consequences of their proposed solutions.

Some community financial institutions are able to meet this challenge. What do they have that makes this possible? A few things.

Purposeful Risk Appetite

Does your bank have the risk appetite to take on the elevated credit, reputational, and legal risk inherent in the type of consumer lending proposed here? You might have 4 to 5 percent of your non-home equity consumer portfolio go delinquent, with little or no collateral. You run the risk that, once you go through an unsuccessful collections process, the bank sells the loan for pennies on the dollar. And then the debt collector uses aggressive tactics to get the money back. Imagine the nightly news reporter broadcasting a spot from that teary-eyed customer's living room.

Transparency can help your financial institution mitigate risk. Start by designing the consumer lending program with a specific end goal in mind. For example, the goal could be to use consumer lending as a tool to grow the wealth of the families the bank serves, at a profit. Assess the demand for such services. Estimate the balances the bank can reasonably generate if successful. Work backwards to calculate the expected profit—given the spread of the balances, fees, and expected losses—to determine the operating expense that would be available to execute on the plan.

Can the bank generate the necessary volume with the available resources? I suggest considering all of consumer lending as one portfolio. Here's why: as with all bank customers and products, some loans will be highly profitable, and others will not. It's not realistic to suggest that one $500 unsecured personal loan would be profitable. But could the entire consumer loan portfolio—one that makes up a meaningful percentage of the entire loan portfolio—be done profitably? I say yes.

This approach suggests that some consumer borrowers will subsidize others. Some will pay too much, while others too little. But how is this different from bank customers as a whole, with their different account balances and needs? If executed properly, the program could help elevate the financial situation of many customers. They could then graduate from being unprofitable to generating sufficient profits to help subsidize other borrowers trying to emerge from the vicious cycle of living paycheck to paycheck.

Some, inevitably, will not. And to mitigate the risk, you must be totally transparent about credit standards, processes, bank responsibilities, and borrower responsibilities. Communicate the ultimate objective of helping families grow wealth while generating enough risk-adjusted return on capital to cover the consumer loan portfolio's cost of capital. Have a clear response prepared for that nightly news interview in a disgruntled customer's living room—even though we all hope it never comes.

Profit is the yardstick that determines whether the bank will keep investing in its employees' capabilities and the technology to continuously improve its offerings. Absence of profit ensures that consumer lending, as a strategic priority, will wither and ultimately die. And that's a lost opportunity for a community financial institution that strives to provide something greater than "accommodation."

Strategic Partnerships

Perhaps consumer lending is indeed outside of your bank's risk appetite. If so, there are ways to reduce risk while still becoming a prominent community resource that meets customers' needs and promotes their financial health. Partnering with a fintech firm or niche bank can help risk-averse banks get to a "yes" in consumer lending.

Figure, for example, is a relatively new consumer lending fintech started by the founder of SoFi. Its primary product was the home equity loan, but it has since expanded into residential mortgage financing and asset management. Figure is one of the first online lending platforms to build its processes on the blockchain to drive down the costs inherent in consumer lending. This is particularly helpful when real estate collateral is involved.

Financial institutions can partner with Figure to build critical mass and geographic diversification in home equity lending. Figure routinely offers a pool of HELOCs for financial institutions to bid on. So instead of starting from a low base, a financial institution can build a portfolio, generate spread, and learn from a forward looking fintech provider on how to drive down cost.

LendingClub, a peer-to-peer lending company founded in 2007, partners with financial institutions in a variety of ways. First, like Figure, it offers financial institutions the ability to purchase loans that meet the bank's underwriting criteria. This can help a bank build critical mass in unsecured personal loans. It can also diversify the bank's loan portfolio by loan type and geography—and shorten the bank's learning curve for building efficiency and managing risk.

LendingClub can also enable banks to co-brand the LendingClub loan application and offer the service to the bank's own customer base. Not only does this digitalize the customer experience, but it also leverages LendingClub's underwriting, risk, and compliance infrastructure. So instead of turning customers away when they need a loan, the bank can strengthen the relationship.

Figure and LendingClub are just two examples of the many partnership opportunities available to community financial institutions for consumer lending. With access to such resources, banks can mitigate the risks associated with consumer lending, gain organizational knowledge, and build critical mass. They can also get back to supporting the essential financial needs of local customers—central to the "community" in a community bank's mission.

Niche Lending

Building a broad-based consumer loan portfolio one borrower at a time is a tough road. Obstacles might include a lack of demand, employee inability to serve as advisors, or a low risk appetite. For many banks, pursuing a lending niche is a more desirable path. This approach can help the bank build focused expertise, achieve geographic portfolio diversity, and target the most likely customers.

1st Security Bank of Washington, in Mountlake Terrace, just north of Seattle, provides traditional community bank loan and deposit services through its 21 branches. Once a credit union, 1st Security became a mutual savings bank, and is now a community bank. Its customers are mostly small- and middle-market businesses and individuals. In addition to its traditional services, it offers three specialty consumer loan niches.

The first niche is indirect home improvement loans—also known as fixture secured loans. As the mainstay of the bank's consumer lending strategy, this niche represents the largest portion of the consumer loan portfolio and 15.6 percent of the gross loan portfolio. Most of the fixture secured loans are originated through 10 dealers, though the network includes over 150 dealers. The loans cover a wide variety of products, such as replacement windows, siding, roofs, HVAC systems, and pools. The second niche is solar loans, which are also fixture secured loans, but specifically for solar related home improvement projects. These loans are originated by the bank through its network of contractors and dealers, and are secured by the personal property installed on the borrower's real property.

Unlike direct loans—where the borrower makes an application directly to the bank—these two niche loans are facilitated by the dealer, who assists the borrower in preparing the loan application. The bank then disburses the loan proceeds directly to the dealer upon receipt of a "completion certificate" signed by the borrower. Because the bank does not have direct contact with the borrower, there is greater risk.

The third niche at 1st Security is marine lending, secured by boats, which the bank does directly with borrowers. These loans are to borrowers in Washington and other states where the bank originates consumer loans.

The entire consumer portfolio at 1ˢᵗ Security represented 23 percent of its total loans, and it yielded 6.87 percent when the Fed Funds Rate was 2.25 percent. Only 21 basis points of its total loan portfolio was non-performing.

But 1ˢᵗ Security Bank of Washington is only one example of niche lending. If you want a menu of options, look to the industrial loan companies (ILC) of Utah. ILCs are special purpose charters that allow commercial companies to own banks. For example, EnerBank USA does unsecured home improvement lending, funded mostly by hot-rate CDs. It made over 2 percent ROA in the most recent year. It is owned by a Michigan energy company—a deep-pocketed holding company that serves as a source of strength to an undiversified bank.

I'm not suggesting you follow EnerBank's business model. But the manner in which it generates significant profits through a niche, nationwide loan product is instructive. As is the manner in which other ILCs drive profits through niche consumer lending.

To Sum It Up...

Consumer lending used to be a material source of interest income and profits for community banks. In recent years, however, regulation, competition, and technology have squeezed smaller institutions out of that line of business. Today, most community banks have yielded the field to large, nationwide lenders and fintech firms. This is a loss, because consumer lending is an area where community financial institutions can make real a difference to their stakeholders.

Some institutions have demonstrated that consumer lending can be done with smaller volumes than one might think. What has helped these banks succeed? Purposeful risk management, strategic partnerships, and focused niche lending. Community bank consumer lending can be done. The question is, do you want to do it?

Points Made This Chapter

❖ In an effort to protect consumers from bad actors in the consumer lending space, regulators have driven good actors out of the business by making it prohibitively expensive and risky.

❖ Consumer lending is central to the mission of most community financial institutions.

❖ By abandoning their consumer lending business, community financial institutions run the risk of losing relevance in their local communities—and potential profits.

❖ Recommendations for bringing consumer loans back to your bank: make them part of your strategy, align your credit culture and risk appetite, drive down costs, and price your loans appropriately.

❖ Another recommendation is to align technology and artificial intelligence with employee capabilities to differentiate your bank from competitors.

❖ The ability to advise customers, increase their financial well-being, and put them on a sustainable wealth building path is essential to community bank consumer lending. A traditional consumer lending strategy without these elements is a hollow, product-centric strategy.

❖ If the bank's risk appetite does not permit booking meaningful volumes of consumer loans, consider partnering with third parties.

❖ To diversify the balance sheet, there are a number of financial institutions that pursue regional or nationwide niche consumer lending.

Section IV

Creating a Valuable Financial Institution

Value is in the eye of the beholder. And the beholder of a financial institution is all of its primary constituents.

Chapter 13

Build a Positive Accountability Culture

How does your financial institution perform compared to the banks down the street? About the same? Do your employees care?

"Peer groups get you to a lazy place," said a bank CEO at a strategic planning retreat. It's important to note that he was warning against focusing on peer averages or medians. Who wants to have: "Here lies John, he was average" as their epithet?

Bankers are clearly interested in relative performance, however. It is a way—perhaps the primary way—to hold executive teams accountable. It provides benchmarks for tracking whether a financial institution is headed in the right direction.

I don't think this topic is relevant only to publicly traded financial institutions. There are millions of investors, including many sophisticated institutional investors, who vote-by-trade for what they think drives value in a financial institution. When we analyze the metrics those investors are looking for, we glean information on how to build something valuable for all stakeholders—customers, employees, and communities, as well as investors. Building and nurturing a positive accountability culture around those metrics—one that rewards achievement and makes course corrections when necessary—should lead to greater profitability. Greater profitability can lead to more attractive rates for customers, greater compensation or benefits for employees, and more significant community contributions. And, yes, better returns for shareholders.

Even if you're not publicly traded, and your other stakeholders are not keeping a close eye on performance, it's risky business to settle for mediocrity. Your financial institution could be creating a laissez faire culture that leads to inefficiencies and wasted resources. Such complacency steals resources from the good the institution can do.

These concerns were likely what drove my articles on performance and value into the top-20. What is considered top performance? What is considered a valuable financial institution? And how should we hold ourselves accountable?

Let's start by looking at what is meant by "top quartile performance."

∞

For Banks, What Is Top Quartile Performance?

January 13, 2018

https://www.jeff4banks.com/2018/01/for-banks-what-is-top-quartile.html

What is top quartile financial performance? I am often asked this question, and top quartile performance appears as stretch goals in many strategic plans. And I say bravo! Nobody wants to be average.

Usually top quartile performance is compared to a bank's or thrift's pre-selected peer group. Executive compensation is often tied to it.

I won't belabor the point. A key benefit of being a blogger is that I can use research I perform for my own knowledge to benefit my readers.

The below statistics are from all FDIC insured financial institutions either for the year-to-date ended or period ended September 30, 2017. This period end was largely driven by the significant number of financial institutions taking deferred tax asset write downs in the fourth quarter, which would have skewed ROAA/ROAE for the year ended 2017. I used Call Report data, so the calendar year is the fiscal year.

I also excluded extraneous performers by category, as noted in the footnotes of each table. For profitability numbers (ROAA, ROAE), I excluded Subchapter S financial institutions. Quite a large cohort at over 1,900. Sub S bankers can gross up those numbers to come up with their equivalents.

See where your financial institution ranks!

Net Interest Margin (%)

	Banks	Thrifts
Top Quartile	4.04	3.62
Average	3.62	3.22
Median	3.66	3.22
Bottom Quartile	3.27	2.85

*Excludes banks/thrifts >5%
Statistics are YTD September 30, 2017
Source: S&P Global Market Intelligence

Efficiency Ratio (%)

	Banks	Thrifts
Top Quartile	58.55	66.34
Average	66.52	73.77
Median	66.50	74.93
Bottom Quartile	75.01	83.55

*Excludes banks/thrifts >100% and <20%
Statistics are YTD September 30, 2017
Source: S&P Global Market Intelligence

Non-Interest Expense/Avg. Assets (%)

	Banks	Thrifts
Top Quartile	2.30	2.26
Average	2.77	2.79
Median	2.74	2.76
Bottom Quartile	3.19	3.24

*Excludes banks/thrifts >5% and <1%
Statistics are YTD September 30, 2017
Source: S&P Global Market Intelligence

NPAs/Avg. Assets (%)

	Banks	Thrifts
Top Quartile	0.23	0.34
Average	1.12	1.24
Median	0.70	0.77
Bottom Quartile	1.43	1.55

*Excludes banks/thrifts >20%
Statistics are YTD September 30, 2017
Source: S&P Global Market Intelligence

Return On Avg. Assets (%)

	Banks	Thrifts
Top Quartile	1.11	0.82
Average	0.90	0.65
Median	0.88	0.58
Bottom Quartile	0.66	0.39

*Excludes banks/thrifts that are Sub S, unprofitable,
and >3%
Statistics are YTD September 30, 2017
Source: S&P Global Market Intelligence

Return On Avg. Equity (%)

	Banks	Thrifts
Top Quartile	10.03	7.17
Average	8.04	5.45
Median	7.91	4.77
Bottom Quartile	5.82	2.94

*Excludes banks/thrifts that are Sub S, unprofitable,
and >25%
Statistics are YTD September 30, 2017
Source: S&P Global Market Intelligence

~ Jeff

∞

So you have a number of useful metrics to consider. But if you're aiming for something better than mediocrity, where should you be setting the bar?

For financial institutions that have or want this level of executive accountability, I suggest two approaches. The first is to look at the median performance for two distinct peer groups: one your current peer and the other your aspirational peer. This accountability mechanism may be best suited for your purposes if you are migrating from your current business model to a different one. The second approach is to use top quartile performance in a few select metrics. If you want to remain in your current business model, but improve your execution of it, perhaps aiming for top quartile performance is the right way to go.

Your Aspirational Peer

A bank I once worked with was transforming its business model from that of a traditional thrift to one that offered commercial bank services. Not uncommon in an environment where retail products are becoming more commoditized and retail banking more regulated. At the start of this journey, the board and executives did not think it would be fair to hold executives accountable to the performance of the banks they aspired to be like. At least not initially.

So during strategic planning, they compared their bank to two peers. The first was a group of banks in their region, of similar size, with similar balance sheet compositions. This was their current peer. It made no sense for this bank to strive toward top quartile performance for its existing peer group. After all, the bank would be focused on its planned strategic shift to a different model.

The executives then laid out the strategy to become more like a commercially focused community bank. It included a hoped-for fundamental transition of their balance sheet. They proposed no longer booking all their residential mortgages—planning instead to increase secondary market activity. Their plan was to recruit teams of commercial bankers to help grow their commercial loans and deposits, thereby leveraging their ample capital with higher yielding, and presumably higher profit products.

Next, they identified the banks they would want to look like if their plans succeeded. Which financial institutions had their hoped-for balance sheet, and drove greater profits? They selected a group and dubbed it their aspirational peer. They tracked their progress in plan execution, in part, by how well they progressed from their current peer medians to their aspirational peer medians.

Would such an accountability tool work for your financial institution?

Top Quartile Performance

The second method for building positive and measurable accountabilities—at least at the executive level—is to achieve top quartile performance as compared to peers in select metrics. This is particularly appropriate if your financial institution's strategy doesn't call for material changes in balance sheet composition. It simply wants to build a culture of continuous improvement.

This can be executed simply. For example, the board of directors, as part of the bank's strategic planning, identifies top quartile performance in ROA, ROE, net interest margin (NIM), and efficiency ratio as signals of success. Incentive compensation can then be based on the bank's ascent from peer average—or wherever the bank is on the peer spectrum—to top quartile. And not all metrics have to be equal. The bank may fall short on NIM, for example, but still achieve top quartile ROA and ROE.

Depending on the bank's strategy, there could be valid reasons for achieving some metrics and not others. Consider a bank that has chosen a differentiation strategy, striving for superior customer service. What if it can't achieve a pricing advantage in the form of a superior NIM, so it gets there by slashing expenses? This might ring the ROA and ROE bell, but not necessarily be true to the strategy. It might help to have sub-goals such as NIM or yield on earning assets or cost of funds. They might indicate how true you are staying to strategy. So be careful not to discount how your institution achieves its targets. Bottom line profitability isn't everything. The journey matters.

A positive accountability culture that is built to last will reach beyond the executive team. Push accountabilities as deep into the organization as possible. Part of the incentive could be based on how well the institution does in its "top of the house" financials compared to its peers. But you should also be thinking about how the branch managers impact net interest margin and ROE at the branch level. What does achieving top quartile net interest margin and ROE mean to them?

That question leads to another critical point. Your management reporting should be designed to be consistent with organizational goals. For a branch, achieving bank-wide top quartile NIM status means the branch managers should be held accountable for continuous improvement in the deposit spreads for their branches. Imagine a bank that has 20 branches, and ranks branch performance by deposit spread, spread trend, spread growth, or other factors consistent with strategy. Now imagine that managers' incentive compensation rewards success. So long as the branch managers are trained to know how to press the levers to improve spread—and have organizational support to help them— accountability can run on autopilot. And the resulting culture should improve spreads, and therefore NIM, at every level.

Similarly, a bank that strives for top quartile ROE can hold lenders accountable for achieving an ROE hurdle in their portfolios. This management reporting should reflect the allocation of capital to each loan based on the perceived risk of that loan type. (See Chapter 5 on RAROC for more on this and the risk adjusted profitability of deposits and loans.)

These days, a significant part of a lender's incentive compensation is typically based on volume. But is this incentive scheme consistent with an institution's strategy of achieving top quartile NIM and ROE? If lenders are held accountable for growing ROE above a specific hurdle rate, you will create strategic alignment that motivates your lenders to work toward peer top quartile, rather than against it. So often, officer loan committees have to contend with the lender who brings in larger yet thinly priced deals. The CEO or CFO likely whines about pricing, but the lender says, "This is the price we need to get the deal done." It doesn't have to be that way.

I'm not saying those conversations will stop. But by focusing on ROE rather than volume, at least you won't be incenting your lenders to continuously repeat them.

Financial Performance That Creates Value

Which "select" metrics do you use? This comes down to strategy. Say your bank believes it has a Ritz-Carlton-like brand. In that case, having a higher yield on loans or lower cost of funds is consistent with higher price points for the brand you built and the service levels you provide. If you're pursuing a cost advantage, on the other hand, perhaps non-interest expense to average assets or efficiency ratio would be appropriate metrics.

There are other considerations, too, such as focusing on metrics that also build the greatest value. When I say "greatest value," I'm talking about the ways outsiders perceive and place value on your institution.

That was the basis for my article on bank value, which attracted a lot of attention. Because the story reflects a spot in time, the details on the five featured financial institutions are not so instructive. What we do need to understand—as much so now as then—are the particular metrics that analysts perceive as creating the most value for shareholders. These metrics, I contend, create value for all stakeholders.

∞

A Bank Analyst Makes Recommendations. I Make a List.

June 28, 2018

https://www.jeff4banks.com/2018/06/a-bank-analyst-makes-recommendations-i.html

What should you look for in a bank stock?

How should I know? I'm not a financial advisor. I would have to take a test to prove that I am worthy of such predictions.

But I read. And part of my reading includes Boenning & Scattergood's quarterly Bank DCF Analysis. In the report, analysts Matt Schultheis and Scott Beury laid down the criteria they recommend investors use when evaluating bank stocks:

1. **Superior Growth Prospects**
2. **Excess Capital**
3. **Strong Deposit Franchises**

Well, ok then Matt and Scott. I'll search on that.

I sorted all publicly traded US banks on the following criteria: year over year asset growth (2016-17) greater than 10%, tangible equity/tangible assets greater than 9%, and CD's as a percent of total deposits less than 30%. I also filtered out banks with greater than 2%

non-performing assets/assets.

This netted a total of 78 banks ranging in asset size from $113 million (Republic Bank of Arizona) to $44 billion (Signature Bank). No SIFI banks.

I then set out to single out the best bank in a few of the categories. The first was for growth, as measured by year over year asset growth. I skipped banks that grew via acquisition during that time. The second was to highlight the most favorable deposit mix, as determined by the lowest level of CDs. I know this is imperfect. There could be ample municipal deposits in checking or money market accounts. Not an ideal funding source but also not CDs.

The third category was performance judged by their first quarter 2018 ROA. Again, not ideal. But directionally correct. The fourth was value based on the bank's price/tangible book. Most of the 78 financial institutions were below $1 billion in total assets. Investors tend to favor price/book metrics in looking at smaller institutions. The lower the multiple, the more value that might be on the table for the investor.

The last category was a balanced approach between all of the measurements I used, including EPS growth. There was judgement involved and I must admit I tended to discount the smaller financial institutions because of their low trading volumes and inefficient valuations. Personal bias, I know. My apologies to Metro Phoenix Bank ($181 million in assets, 1.88%/11.83% ROA/ROE).

The results are in the table below.

	Growth	Deposit Mix	Best For Performance	Value	Balance*
	MCB	IIBK	SBT	FSDK	BOCH
Total Assets ($000)	1,968,886	698,827	3,034,332	280,804	1,245,575
Asset Growth Rate (2016-17)	44%	12%	37%	12%	11%
Tang. Eq./Tang. Assets (%)	13.0%	9.5%	9.2%	13.9%	9.9%
CDs/Tot. Deposits (%)	5.7%	2.8%	29.6%	16.3%	17.2%
NPAs/Assets (%)	0.35%	0.19%	0.12%	0.98%	1.04%
ROAA (%)	1.35%	0.85%	2.13%	0.59%	1.04%
ROAE (%)	10.53%	8.55%	22.17%	4.23%	10.20%
EPS Growth (CAGR 2015-1Q18)	34%	6%	49%	39%	12%
Price/EPS (x)	17.6	20.3	11.3	17.8	15.6
Price/Tang. Book (%)	190.2%	163.7%	250.2%	75.9%	162.2%
Dividend Yield (%)	NA	NA	0.3%	2.4%	1.3%

*Jeff For Banks weighting of B&S categories, plus valuation, favoring larger FI's.

NOT AN INVESTMENT RECOMMENDATION

Source: S&P Global Market Intelligence

MCB - Metropolitan Bank Holding Corp., New York, NY

IIBK - Idaho Independent Bank, Coeur d'Alene, ID

SBT - Sterling Bancorp, Inc., Southfield, MI

FSDK - First Citizens National Bank of Upper Sandusky, Upper Sandusky, OH

BOCH - Bank of Commerce Holding, Sacramento, CA

Who else should be on the list?

~ Jeff

∞

Let's take a closer look at those three criteria for value creation.

Superior Growth Prospects

"Superior growth prospects" can be interpreted multiple ways. If we're considering asset growth, what would be the path of least resistance to achieving it? In the 1990s there were many more mutually owned financial institutions than there are today. And mutual-to-stock conversions were frequent. The growth trajectory for those banks was far more dramatic than we normally expect these days. That's because a mutual has no shareholders. Its capital is built up slowly over time, through retained earnings—and mutuals generally hold more capital than shareholder-owned institutions. So when a mutual converts to a shareholder-owned institution, it sells shares first to depositors, then to the public, and usually winds up with significant over-capitalization.

As a result, these former mutuals went about putting that capital to work. Since that level of rapid growth would be difficult to achieve prudently in the loan portfolio, these banks leveraged their newly found and ample capital by buying investment securities on their asset side. They would fund the purchases with a combination of the new capital and wholesale borrowings on the liability side. In other words, they grew rapidly. In some cases, exponentially. And it was almost overnight. The path of least resistance to them was a couple of phone calls.

Is this the type of value-building superior growth contemplated by the bank stock analysts? Asset growth can be achieved in many ways. And not always in valuable ways. Today there are other ways to assess growth potential that are more helpful.

Many financial institutions believe premium pricing can be achieved by focusing on clients who place value on service and relationships—and by delivering on the value proposition. If this is the case at your institution, then top quartile NIM could be an aspirational metric. Some financial institutions, however, do not. They may believe Ritz-Carlton service gives them more at-bats, keeps customers longer, and builds deeper relationships. But for them, superior growth prospects don't necessarily equate to top quartile NIM. Superior growth should, however, equate to top quartile net interest income growth. And maybe that's their flavor of superior growth prospects.

Peter Lynch, the legendary 1980s-90s fund manager for the Fidelity Magellan fund, touted the PEG ratio—the price to earnings ratio divided by earnings growth. He felt that a company, any company, whose PEG ratio was one was fairly valued. Set aside for a moment the fact that financial institutions are required to have a relatively high amount of capital, which makes this formula problematic. The underlying concept of earnings growth as a proxy for superior growth prospects can be helpful.

Using earnings growth instead of asset, loan, or even deposit growth has a couple of benefits. First, it takes into account—at least partially—the amount of risk a financial institution takes to achieve growth. If it adds riskier loans, the institution must put more in its loan loss provision, thereby reducing earnings. This metric is particularly useful for institutions whose stakeholders value them by looking at long-term performance. As Warren Buffett once said, "Only when the tide goes out do you discover who's been swimming naked." In other words, a recession usually uncovers the amount of risk in a balance sheet.

Second, earnings growth also demonstrates how well a management team achieves economies of scale as it grows. Adding the next $100 million of additional assets should cost less than the previous $100 million. So growing the balance sheet at 5 percent—at an institution with operating discipline—should result in greater than 5 percent growth in earnings. In addition to delivering greater value to shareholders, earnings can also fund increased employee development, investments in technology and the customer experience, and community support.

Excess Capital

See Chapter 5 for how to determine whether you have excess capital, and some ideas on where to deploy it. If you do find your institution with excess capital, based on calculations from the ground up, it may be time to "pull into the pits."

In auto racing, cars whip around an oval track until they need gas, tires, or maintenance to give them what they need to stay competitive during the race. Similarly, companies need to pull into the pits occasionally to get their version of gas and tires. Physical expansion into nearby geographies or technology investments to expand concentric circles around branches are ways a bank can reasonably gain market share.

Pulling into the pits could also mean internal process reviews, ensuring that existing technology is used to its fullest capacity and inefficient or ineffective processes are modified or eliminated. Or it could be team development, improving the abilities of existing employees or adding more employees to fuel the next level of growth.

For most institutions, a pit stop is likely a combination of many things. And the bank may face the immediate impact of slowed growth or decreased earnings—much as a race car risks losing position when it makes a pit stop. The decrease in earnings, purposefully orchestrated to increase capacity for the next leg of growth, is a means to use excess capital. Excess capital drives value by providing dry powder to grow faster than the institution's internal capital generation—or to weather the storm of a recession. If the bank is comfortable with the latter, then it should position itself for the former.

Whether you're shareholder owned or not, this strategy should be transparent to all stakeholders: To your shareholder, who might see multiple quarters of declining earnings and/or reduced capital ratios. To your customers, who might experience disruption as you implement new technologies. To your employees tasked with executing in the pits, to ensure they understand and move toward your planned outcome…positioning the institution for future growth.

Strong Deposit Franchises

Over the past twenty years, I have measured the price to book and price to tangible book trading multiples of community financial institutions, based on who had the top quartile yield on earning assets versus who had the top quartile cost of funds (meaning lowest cost of funds). In all but one instance, the banks with the lower cost of funds traded at higher market multiples. Why?

The answer is borne out in the Boenning and Scattergood research cited above. The preference for superior growth prospects, excess capital, and strong deposit franchises, is very common among all bank stock analysts. And investors, it seems, value deposit gathering more than being able to generate loan volume. With twenty-plus years of measuring bank product profitability, I feel comfortable saying that while loans generate profits, it is deposits that generate value.

The reason, as I see it, is that core deposit gathering is more difficult than generating loan volume. It takes about 50 net new business operating accounts to fund one $2 million commercial real estate loan. Experienced bankers know which is more difficult. That is why core funded financial institutions receive favorable market valuations.

Growth prospects, excess capital, and deposit franchises can all be measured through publicly available data. In fact, publicly available data is exactly what I used in the above article. It should be easy for banks to hold themselves accountable to these attributes. It's possible that "excess capital" would be managed only at the executive level. When a financial institution has the operating discipline to allocate capital to business units based on the risks within those units, they should have precisely the right amount of capital in them.

However, accountabilities for achieving superior growth and strong deposit franchises can be done at the most granular levels within the organization. North Fork Bank, a Long Island based institution that was sold to CapitalOne in 2007, calculated lender bonuses primarily from their deposit generation. It had a 2.85 percent cost of funds when the Fed Funds Rate was 5.25 percent. They did it. And so can you.

To Sum It Up...

To cultivate a positive accountability culture at your bank, management should consider implementing a strategy with consistent financial accountabilities that reach throughout the entire organization. If your strategy is to achieve superior net interest margins through deep relationships, for example, you should measure NIM at the top of the house, along with spreads generated within each business unit. If your strategy is to seek cost discipline, you should look for a consistent decline in deposit operations expense as a percent of average deposits. To build a lasting culture consistent with strategy, focus on the wins and reward them. Banks that lead with the stick ultimately get clobbered by it. Lead with the carrot, lift up your people, correct your course when needed, and build an institution to last.

Points Made This Chapter

- ❖ Beware of comparing yourself to the average, because you might end up achieving it.

- ❖ Maintaining accountabilities should benefit all stakeholders: shareholders, customers, employees, and communities. If your bank is not shareholder owned, consider the ways your other stakeholders benefit from superior financial performance.

- ❖ Establish executive accountability by using top quartile performance in a few select metrics. Or use medians of two peer groups: one should be your current peer and the other your aspirational peer.

- ❖ The metrics you compare yourself to should be consistent with your strategy.

- ❖ Buy-side investors believe the best metrics to measure value creation are: superior growth prospects, excess capital, and strong deposit franchises.

- ❖ "Superior growth" begs the question: What are you trying to grow? Instead of focusing on asset growth, consider net interest margin expansion or balance sheet growth—which both lead to net interest income growth—or earnings growth.

- ❖ "Pulling into the pits" is a valid exercise in deploying excess capital. Position the bank for its next leg of growth.

- ❖ Core deposit growth is generally more valued by investors because it is more difficult to achieve than loan growth.

Chapter 14

What Drives Value?

I n the prior chapter, we looked at the financial metrics sought out by bank stock analysts—in other words, the opinions of a few. What of the opinions of the many? And by many, I mean the tens of thousands of bank stock investors who trade millions of bank stock shares every day. En masse, what do they think drives value?

This is essential information for any bank. To build an enduring financial institution—that is, one that's designed to satisfy all of its primary stakeholders—it's necessary to study and implement what those stakeholders are looking for. The rapid pace of M&A in financial services adds a layer of urgency to this need. Any shareholder-owned institution that wishes to remain independent must earn that right. How? By providing the shining light of a great community partner. By delivering a superior customer experience. By becoming one of the best banks to work for. If your bank is perpetually underperforming in metrics that matter, you can bet your stakeholders are hoping you'll be bought up by someone who can do a better job.[xxxviii]

So it's important to recognize that financial metrics are not the only metrics that drive value. But they are absolutely foundational for at least one primary constituency: your shareholders. And you cannot provide value to the rest of your constituents without delivering on the metrics favored by shareholders.

The two articles below, both in the top 20 that I've written, were focused on financial metrics.

∞

For Financial Institutions, What Drives Value?

September 26, 2018

https://www.jeff4banks.com/2018/09/for-financial-institutions-what-drives.html

Not all financial institutions are publicly traded. But there are enough of them to help those that do not trade to measure what metrics drive the value of their franchise.

So what metrics drive value? Umrai Gill, Managing Director of Performance Trust in Chicago presented his findings to the Financial Managers Society at their East Coast Regional Conference this month. Some results were surprising.

He first cited a survey performed by PT, asking their clients "what are the generally accepted drivers of institutional value?" Without identifying ranking or more details about their survey, the preponderance of responses were as follows, in no particular order: loan-to-deposit ratio, investment portfolio size, net interest margin, efficiency ratio, return on average assets (ROAA), return on average tangible equity (ROATE), capitalization, and asset size.

Some were not very interesting to me, such as investment portfolio size, which might have been influenced by PT's specialty. Others might have been too investment community-like, such as ROATE, which doesn't count high premiums bank buyers pay for bank sellers that results in goodwill on the buyers' books, which is deducted from their regulatory capital. But others struck my curiosity to see if there were correlations between the metric and market valuations.

And I thought I would share with my readers. The charts in the slides below was PT's analysis of data from S&P Global Market Intelligence based on June 30, 2018 financial information using market data from 08/17/18.

First, the metrics that showed correlation to price to tangible book values. Not surprising, in my opinion.

Asset Size

Median Price / Tangible Book Value by Total Assets

Efficiency Ratio

Median Price / Tangible Book Value by Efficiency Ratio

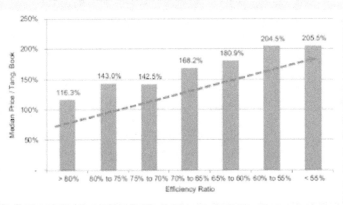

Profitability / ROAA

Median Price / Tangible Book Value by ROAA

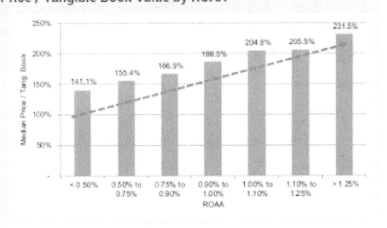

Next, the ratio that did not show a correlation to price to tangible book multiples, at least not over 3.5%. I was a little surprised at this one.

Net Interest Margin

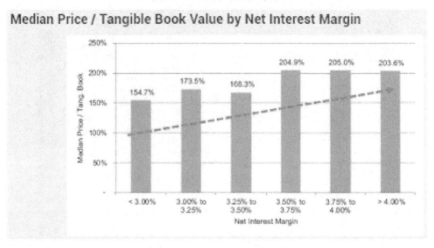

Median Price / Tangible Book Value by Net Interest Margin

Lastly, and most interesting from my point of view, were ratios that showed mixed results. In other words, they showed positive correlation to price-to-tangible book ratios, up to a point. After which, they showed a correlation, but not what bankers would hope for.

Tangible Common Equity / Tangible Assets

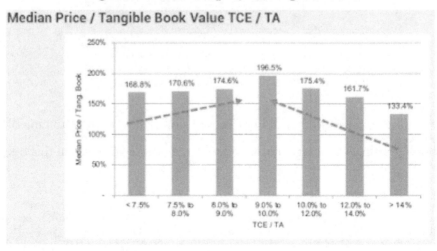

Median Price / Tangible Book Value TCE / TA

Loan-to-Deposit Ratio

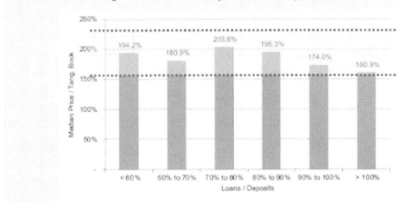

The highest market multiples were afforded to banks with a 70%-80% loan to deposit ratio. Now that may be related to size of institution, as the very largest, JPMorgan Chase (67% loan/deposit ratio) and Wells Fargo (76%) tend to have lower ratios. But there is likely something to the fact that a bank that still has strong liquidity as represented by a relatively lower loan-to-deposit ratio in a good economy has room to improve earnings by growing loans faster than deposits. While the less liquid must price up their deposits to get funding.

And capital, well, I refer you to a prior post where I clearly stated there was such a thing as too much capital. Investors will not pay a premium for hoarded capital. Performance Trust's research puts that sweet spot in the 9%-10% tangible common equity / tangible assets range. Enough capital to grow and/or absorb recessionary losses without selling off assets at a discount to bolster capital during hard times.

Where are your sweet spots?

~ Jeff

∞

My next article on financial metrics that drive value was based on a question asked by a reader. I thought the answer to his question would benefit all readers, so I published it as a separate item, shortly after the first piece. Consider it a follow-on to the one above.

∞

For Financial Institutions, What Drives Value v2

October 9, 2018

https://www.jeff4banks.com/2018/10/financial-institutions-what-drives.html

In a follow up to my last post on the subject, that was driven by my friends from Performance Trust, I was asked in the comments section of that post if there was a correlation between non-interest bearing checking accounts and price-to-tangible book multiples.

That nugget was asked by Mike Higgins, a bank consultant from Kansas City, who penned a guest post on these pages in the past. Rather than answer Mike in the comments, I opted for the wider audience distribution of a standalone post.

It's my blog. I can do what I want.

I am somewhat limited to how financial institutions report their deposit mix. Call report categories are easiest, and the closest metric is transaction accounts to total deposits. I thought this would give us what we needed.

So, is there a correlation between a bank's relative level of transaction accounts to their price-to-tangible book trading multiple?

See for yourself.

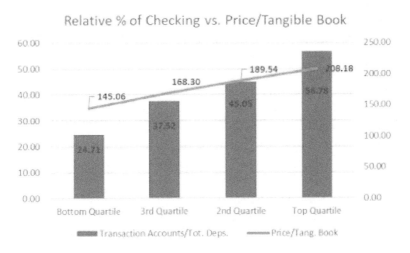

The data, courtesy of S&P Global Market Intelligence, is all publicly traded US banks with trading volumes greater than 1,000 shares per day, and that have non-performing assets to total assets less than 2%. That filtered out most of the very small, inefficiently traded financial institutions, and those with asset quality issues. I also eliminated banks that had NA in the transaction accounts/total deposits ratio.

The filters resulted in 306 financial institutions, which I divvied up into quartiles based on transaction accounts to total deposits. The top quartile, with 56.78% transaction accounts to total deposits traded at 208% price to tangible book at market close on October 4, 2018. The bottom quartile, with 24.71% transaction accounts to total deposits, traded at 145% price to tangible book. The line is linear. Which reads funny as I proofread.

So I would say: yes, community bank investors reward banks funded with a higher proportion of checking accounts with greater trading multiples. So when I wrote in June 2018, in a post titled Branch Talk, my point [xxxix] was that banks needed to build a cost of funds advantage by having a relatively higher proportion of checking accounts, the above chart is why.

In reviewing the data that fed the above chart, size was likely not a significant issue. All of the numbers above are medians, not averages. And the median asset size from bottom quartile to top were: $1.6B, $2.2B, $3.2B, $2.1B. Wells Fargo and JPMorgan, the nation's largest FIs, were both in the 3rd quartile.

A bonus table:

	Bottom Quartile	3rd Quartile	2nd Quartile	Top Quartile
ROAA	1.00	1.04	1.16	1.25
P/EPS	13.8	14.8	14.4	15.3

So there is a neat line in Return on Average Assets too. Price to earnings is not so neat, but I find it rarely is. Still, the message is clear. More checking, better performance, higher trading multiples.

Do you see it differently?

~ Jeff

∞

Do you think you're immune from worrying about what investors would think about your institution? You're not. Delivering on the performance metrics that have a high correlation to higher trading multiples is part of any bank's recipe for resisting acquisition. This is true even if you don't trade. Even if you're not shareholder owned. After all, mutually owned institutions and credit unions merge too, even though there is no financial consideration conferred to the seller.

If you are shareholder owned but not publicly traded, you likely have your shares valued by an outside professional from time to time. This is a common procedure for share repurchases, benefit plans such as stock options and/or grants, and employee stock option plans. The outside firm will compare your performance to that of multiple peers to place a value on your shares. If delivering on financial metrics is important to the investment community, that should result in higher valuations in this process.

Furthermore, if you are publicly traded, a higher valuation gives you great currency to acquire other institutions. Especially vulnerable are the banks that are not performing at the same level as you and not enjoying those trading multiples. That's because you can offer the seller more on a nominal per-share basis than competing buyers that do not trade at your levels. Another advantage: Positioning yourself as a highly valued buyer gives your institution the opportunity to spread your culture of balancing resources to benefit all primary stakeholders. Certainly more so than underperforming financially and trading below your potential. That will only make you vulnerable to being bought and adopting the buyer's culture. If your culture is worth keeping, then earn the right to keep it.

Contrarian Thinking

I should note that when I wrote those articles on value metrics, the Fed Funds Rate was 2 percent and rising. The value of deposits was emerging from the doldrums caused by the Fed's years-long zero percent position following the 2008 financial crisis. Remember, when the low end of the yield curve is at or near zero, it is difficult for financial institutions to turn profits with deposit products. Branches also struggle. With that in mind, consider the data that show a positive correlation between core deposits and price to tangible book ratios. Will that correlation remain true in a rate environment where the low end of the yield curve is near zero?

In a zero-rate environment, large financial institutions look critically at their branch network. The decline in number of branches at big banks started in 2009. Rates were zero, and branch profitability reports had been bleeding red ink. There had been a branch boom in the mid to late 1990s and into the 2000s, so the country was due for a correction. And low deposit branches weren't cutting it because there simply was not enough revenue, i.e. deposit spread, flowing through them.

Community financial institutions might consider a similar discipline as they become more sophisticated at measuring branch and deposit product profitability. Increasingly, they are basing decisions on data analysis rather than anecdotes. Hard data to make hard decisions.

I say this despite the numerous times I've analyzed the trading multiples of top quartile (meaning lowest) cost-of-funds banks against the trading multiples of top quartile yield-on-earning-assets banks. Almost every time, the lowest cost-of-funds banks traded at higher price to book ratios. The one exception was in 2012, when the Fed Funds Rate happened to be... you guessed it, zero.

However, there is never a bad time to acquire core deposits. I would take that statement even further to say that a low-rate environment is an ideal time for community banks to aggressively pursue core deposits. That's because, when core deposits are least profitable, the largest financial institutions won't be pursuing them. Big banks already own tremendous deposit market share, even in markets where they don't have branches. This strategy may not help your bank expand net interest margin, but it might help grow revenue in the form of net interest income and fee income. Plus, it could position your bank for long-term success. Once the economy has emerged from a zero-rate environment, your short-term-thinking competitors will start anew at pursuing core depositors. But you will have already won them.

Non-Financial Metrics

If there is one prevailing theme I ask you to take away from this book, it would be "positive accountability culture." A culture where wins are celebrated in companywide award ceremonies. Where supervisors take notice when they catch employees doing something right. Where one "aww crap" doesn't have the power to wipe out 10 "atta boys," as it did in my Navy days. That "aww crap" should be viewed as an opportunity to learn rather than the chance to point a finger. When a bank genuinely focuses on the positive, constructive criticism has greater impact. That's because the person delivering the criticism has greater credibility and is more likely to be trusted by the colleague receiving the criticism. Positive accountability, however, need not be limited to financial metrics in the institution's Call Reports or management reporting.

Accountability can also apply to corporate strategy. For example, what if part of your strategy is to accelerate job creation in your communities to spur economic growth? You could measure job growth from the time the strategy was adopted to track progress and maintain accountabilities. In using this broad metric in support of one of your primary stakeholders—your communities—you could implement strategic initiatives to achieve just that.

These initiatives could include creating and managing a community angel investment fund to award equity capital to the most promising businesses. It could include training bank employees to serve as job transition counselors who connect members of the community to vocational resources. That way, banks in communities that depend on dying industries could be part of the solution for retraining an at-risk workforce to become qualified for the jobs of the future. Another initiative could include concentrated giving to charitable organizations focused on job creation and economic growth. The point is, the initiatives would be designed to meet the non-financial metric of job creation. And if initiatives fail to deliver on that metric, the bank should make corrections.

Some financial institutions recognize the importance of employees to the organization's success, and hold themselves accountable for employee quality and retention. They may track, for example, how many positions are filled from within rather from the outside. This is a significant metric because inside hiring signals to the entire staff that the institution is committed to the development and career advancement of its people. A bank that's committed to "keeping the keepers" (see Chapter 1) should also measure tenure trends for employees rated "above average" and higher on periodic evaluations. Imagine an awards ceremony where the CEO hands a "Keep the Keepers" trophy to the assistant vice president of deposit operations for having the most improved tenure trend. That could be one heck of a year-end party.

To Sum It Up...

To achieve long-term value, a financial institution's strategic initiatives should be designed to satisfy all of its primary stakeholders: employees, customers, communities, and shareholders. And those strategic initiatives should be in a symbiotic balance: Great employees lead to a great customer experience. A superior customer experience leads to differentiation in a commoditized industry. Differentiation leads to greater financial performance—which in turn gives the institution the resources to move communities forward.

Is your institution on track? Look at the metrics that drive value. Align them with your vision and mission. And maintain positive accountabilities at all levels. Simple accountabilities. In an environment where banks are being acquired nearly every week, you need to earn your right to remain independent. And you can't do that without creating a valuable financial institution.

Points Made In This Chapter

❖ Every day, tens of thousands of bank stock investors tell the story of what drives value in a financial institution.

❖ A bank's value should be considered through the lenses of all primary constituents, not just the shareholders.

❖ You cannot provide value to the rest of your constituents without delivering on the metrics favored by shareholders. This holds true whether the institution is shareholder owned or not.

❖ There is a correlation between the relative level of non-interest bearing checking accounts and price-to-tangible book multiples.

❖ If you are shareholder owned, higher valuations give you great currency to acquire other institutions and deliver to an even greater number of employees, customers, and communities.

❖ There is never a bad time to grow core deposits.

❖ To measure how well the institution drives value to customers, employees, and communities, implement easily tracked and understood non-financial metrics.

Chapter 15

The Real Reason for Scale

"Get big or get out." How often do we hear talking heads say something like this? So often that I know bankers who have become wary of having institutional investors parroting this message in their boardrooms. So often, in fact, that when I published my observations on bank scale, bankers visited the story by the thousands.

Every FDIC-insured bank reports its financial performance and condition quarterly. And that's publicly available information. So bankers are in the habit—and rightly so—of comparing their financial performance to others. In my discussion of accountability culture, I quote a bank CEO who believes that peer groups move us to a lazy place. And I agree that comparing yourself to peer averages motivates you to perform, well, slightly above average.

But there is no doubt that bankers running smaller, highly profitable community banks must feel crestfallen when larger banks with laggard performance receive higher values in the market.

Here's what I originally published on this phenomenon.

∞

The Real Reason for Bank Scale: Trading Multiples

https://www.jeff4banks.com/2018/08/the-real-reason-for-bank-scale-trading.html

August 25, 2018

"Get big or get out." "You must be twice the size that you are to succeed." These are bromides that some industry talking heads might be telling you. I hear it and read it frequently. And in today's social media, non fact-based opinion society, if you say it enough, people may start to believe it.

I moderated a strategic planning retreat with a bank that achieved top quartile financial performance. Their growth was solid too. Their asset size was less than $500 million. A director challenged me: Does our size matter so long as we continue to perform the way we have performed? My answer: Not really, with one exception.

Trading multiples. I referenced this phenomenon in a 2013 blog post, Too Small to Succeed in Banking.[xl] In that post I opined, "As we migrate towards greater institutional ownership, stock liquidity is becoming increasingly important." What I said then likely remains true today. Institutional owners (funds, etc.) now own two-thirds of shares outstanding in publicly traded US banks.

But why does this matter to my sub $500 million in assets bank client?

So I ran some charts for you (courtesy of S&P Global Market Intelligence).

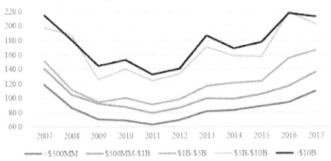

Price to Tang. Book Multiples by Bank Asset Size

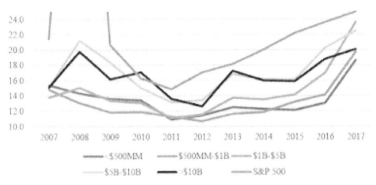

Price to Earnings Multiples by Bank Asset Size

Percent of S&P 500 P/E

	<$500MM	$500MM- $1B	$1B-$5B	$5B-$10B	>$10B
2007	71.8%	69.1%	64.3%	70.1%	70.3%
2008	20.2%	18.5%	21.3%	30.0%	27.9%
2009	65.8%	57.3%	64.7%	88.8%	78.1%
2010	82.4%	73.0%	80.3%	92.3%	104.8%
2011	73.4%	76.0%	74.9%	88.6%	91.6%
2012	67.1%	62.9%	67.8%	78.8%	74.1%
2013	68.9%	64.1%	75.7%	92.5%	94.9%
2014	61.3%	59.2%	67.6%	80.5%	79.8%
2015	54.7%	59.6%	63.8%	72.6%	71.6%
2016	55.3%	59.9%	71.9%	85.9%	79.7%
2017	74.8%	79.2%	94.8%	90.1%	80.4%
Medians	67.1%	62.9%	67.8%	85.9%	79.7%

The bottom table was a bonus so readers can see that at the end of 2017 bank p/e's relative to the S&P 500 p/e surpassed their 10-year median in every asset category. Significantly so for banks $500 million to $5 billion in assets. So, on a relative basis, valuations are higher. 2008 was an anomaly because the S&P 500 companies traded at stratospheric p/e's because they had no "e".

Back to my main point. Over the past 10 years, banks that have less than $500 million in total assets have traded at lower price-to-tangible book multiples. In every year. And the differences in multiples match up nicely by asset size. The price-to-earnings chart is a little murkier based on the choppiness of earnings. However, investors tend to value smaller financial institutions more on book value than earnings. A good earner, like my client, tend to trade at relatively low p/e's because they have great earnings.

Does that sound right? Earn better, and get rewarded with a lower p/e?

Fair is in the eye of the beholder. If you remove nearly 2/3 of the potential shareholder base because you have little daily trading volume, then you have less buyers seeking your shares. Supply and demand.

And that is where the economies of scale argument has merit. If you intend to remain independent, and continue to perform well and grow sufficiently, then you are likely delivering total returns acceptable to shareholders. Even without trading multiple expansion.

But if you would like to acquire a nearby financial institution, and you are trading at lower trading multiples than other would-be acquirers, you would be at a disadvantage. Your "currency" isn't worth as much as your larger competitors. Which may also make you vulnerable to an aggressive buyer's offer to buy you, if the buyer is large and has much better trading multiples than your bank.

Fortunately, unsolicited offers are not common in our cordial industry. But we shouldn't rely on it.

~ Jeff

∞

The takeaway: a nationwide—no, worldwide—movement away from ownership of individual stocks to investing in funds has had an adverse effect on small community banks.

Complicating matters, many small banks are family-owned. Next generation owners are not always interested in retaining a piece of the community bank headquartered in the town where they grew up. Often enough, they've gone away to college and moved out.

In many ways, this type of attitude is short-sighted. The dividends from these small yet profitable banks sustained the owners' families and helped pay for their kids to go to college. So it seems a shame when the heirs cast aside the "spoon that fed 'em" for the instant gratification of a big-city house paid for by the sale of that same bank stock.

But in other ways, the heirs are right. There is less and less demand to

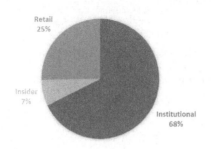

Source: *S&P Global Market Intelligence*

own the stock of a smaller community bank. Institutional funds are not particularly interested in the stock of a bank that has little trading volume. Some have rules preventing such investments. How would they trade in and out of it? The accompanying chart exemplifies the challenge. In 2006, prior to the financial crisis, institutional investors owned 51 percent of publicly traded financial institutions. In 2010, after the crisis, they owned 62 percent. Today it's 68 percent.

Many of these institutional funds now require their portfolio companies to focus not just on the shareholder but other stakeholders too. In fact, the business corporation laws in most states call on boards and managements to give similar weight to customers, employees, communities and shareholders when making decisions. Not all states mind you. But most. And if you've read this book all the way up to this chapter, you know that I do too.

This is a positive development. But is it sustainable? Fund managers, after all, are accountable for performance. The almighty spreadsheet continues to reign. And many funds that specialize in bank stock investing are sub-advisors to larger funds. Imagine that sub-advisor telling the large fund manager that they didn't have a good year—but, hey, many of their portfolio companies raised their employee minimum wage. Mixed-bag performance doesn't play well as you move up the food chain. So I'm a little skeptical of the emerging altruism of institutional investors. But I'm nonetheless thankful for what there is of it. And serving all stakeholders equally need not be a zero-sum game.

If the trend towards institutional ownership continues—and I anticipate it will—then community banks with low trading volume need greater scale to achieve more trading volume.

There are exceptions. A publicly traded financial institution near my home has $1.3 billion in assets and only 21 percent institutional ownership. Its stock trades at about thirteen thousand shares per day. That's a lot—as a general rule, smaller financial institutions have a greater proportion of retail shareholders, who don't trade at the same volume levels as institutional investors.

Of course, retail shareholders should be cultivated differently than institutional investors. In the banking space, you can probably see all the institutional investors you need by attending three or four institutional investor road shows put on by the usual suspects. (I joke with some bank CFOs about the name of the institutional investor rep who calls you quarterly to discuss performance. If the rep's name is Cody, you're probably not as high on the fund's radar. Please no calls or nasty e-mails from anyone named Cody.)

The retail shareholder requires a different approach. Many, if not most, will put much more weight behind the ten college scholarships you awarded to local high school kids than the institutional shareholder will. So the contents of your slide deck will depend on which group you're presenting to.

How you communicate will also vary, depending on your audience.

Retail investors outnumber their institutional counterparts, even if they own a smaller proportion of your shares. Make an effort to know who they are as a group. Are there demographic similarities among them? Can you perform an analysis on their geography and psychographic categories? Develop a game plan to communicate with them at the level that will be most effective. I have suggested quarterly cocktail receptions that include a brief presentation on performance. This provides a good forum for reporting on ways the institution has served all of its stakeholders, plus it's an opportunity for a meet-and-greet between shareholders and bank management. Most communities enjoy a good cocktail party—with a few probable exceptions, like the Amish-focused bank headquartered near me. Again, it pays to know who your investors are.

Be aware, though: a good relationship with your retail investors doesn't let you off the hook with institutional investors. Even if you have a larger proportion of retail shareholders—and a plan to keep them engaged, interested, and invested—you're unlikely to stop the trend towards institutional ownership. Think of your own personal finances. How much do you have in funds—via your IRA, 401k, etc.—versus in individual stocks? The train has left the station. You must have viable alternatives to your retail shareholders. And those alternatives require liquidity—and therefore trading volume—which usually comes with greater scale.

ESOPs, Beyond the Fables

One way to replenish a declining retail share ownership is through an employee stock ownership plan, or ESOP. That's the approach Old Fort Banking Company in Ohio took in 2015.[xli] At that point, the bank had been owned and operated by the Gillmor family for generations. Dianne Gillmor Krumsee, who was then chairman, owned shares that equated to 45 percent of the company. So when she decided to divest, the bank established an ESOP to buy those shares. Since then, the ESOP has grown to hold 63 percent of the company, which currently has $583 million in total assets, a 1.33 percent ROA, and a 15.8 percent ROE. With financial performance like that, Old Fort has earned its right to remain independent. And now, it also has an outlet to provide stock liquidity to exiting shareholders.

Here's how it works: An ESOP is a trust that serves as a qualified retirement plan, providing employees an ownership interest in their company by investing primarily in stock of the employer. The ESOP is funded with tax-deductible contributions by the employer in the form of company stock. In the case of the Old Fort ESOP, funding comprised cash that was used to purchase company stock—specifically, the chairman's shares. ESOPs can be leveraged—meaning they can borrow to fund share purchases. A New Jersey banker once told me with pride that a number of his bank's long-term employees were millionaires as a result of the ESOP. Imagine that. A bank that turned its rank-and-file employees into millionaires.

An ESOP, however, likely does not solve the challenge of a lower stock valuation that inhibits the financial institution's ability to acquire.

Holding Company Complexities

In an effort to gain the scale necessary for greater trading multiples and increased stock liquidity, some financial institutions form multi-bank holding companies. I've had clients that used this structure. Almost all of them couldn't wait to get out of it. The reason: It causes regulatory headaches. Nobody wants multiple exams per year. You can see how this structure has fallen out of favor, as traditionally high-performing banks like Zions Bancorporation and Glacier Bancorp have abandoned the model and consolidated their charters.

But if you accept the evidence that larger financial institutions enjoy greater stock liquidity and trading multiples, then you have to consider your options. A multi-bank holding company may be a way for your financial institution and others to combine under one umbrella—while keeping your "100 year old" bank status. Recently, banking regulations have loosened somewhat, and the frequency of exams has been reduced. Many operational areas can be put into the holding company, with management contracts between each of the bank subsidiaries driving economies of scale. (See Chapter 6.) At the same time, core customer-facing functions and decisions can remain in each bank.

The multi-bank holding company is not an elegant solution. But it can provide the scale your financial institution lacks. And it can deliver a higher technology spend, greater career advancement opportunities for your personnel, and greater stock liquidity for your shareholders. That, in turn, can entice more institutional owners and higher trading multiples because you are now a larger bank holding company.

To Sum It Up...

I know bankers who don't trust investment bankers in their boardroom because of their "get big or get out" message. Economies of scale is their buzz phrase. But Old Fort Banking Company—and hundreds of other small community financial institutions—deliver superior financial performance and growth that should earn them the right to remain independent.

Banks with $5 billion to $10 billion in total assets, on average, deliver superior financial performance compared to all other size cohorts—even greater than the larger banks. But "on average" is a peculiar term. There are hundreds of exceptions. What's generally consistent, however, is the stock liquidity and trading multiples that accompany a larger financial institution. And in this sense, scale does matter.

Points Made This Chapter

❖ Larger financial institutions trade at higher price to tangible book values compared to smaller ones.

❖ Lower trading multiples put financial institutions at a disadvantage in acquiring other financial institutions.

❖ Institutional ownership of publicly traded financial institutions is large and growing.

❖ Conversely, retail ownership is shrinking—and this trend is likely to continue.

❖ In addition to higher trading multiples and greater stock liquidity, a larger financial institution has more resources for technology spending. And it can provide greater advancement opportunity for personnel.

❖ An ESOP can be a ready buyer of your stock in the absence of institutional buyers.

❖ A multi-bank holding company can give your financial institution scale without erasing your history and culture.

Chapter 16

Banking for Good

U nlike the other chapters in this book, this one was not driven by popular demand for the topic. The article it's based on was not in my top 20 most read. But I wish it was. That's because it describes a bank that gives us a thought-provoking example of the natural evolution of capitalism. Now, I'm sure I don't need to enumerate the virtues of capitalism to an audience of bankers. I will, however, point out the aspects of it that I admire most. I believe it has been the single most successful economic system in terms of its potential to reduce poverty, increase economic mobility, and provide the opportunity for people to live the way they dream of living. That's what I've observed across a long career that spans both banking and military service, around the world and across numerous economic cycles.

And there is no organization better positioned than a financial institution to distribute capital to members of the community, who can then use it to build businesses. To create jobs. To increase or improve housing. To educate the future workforce. Or just to buy a home and start a family. You could think of it as bankers helping neighbors. I think of it as "enlightened self-interest." Empowering neighbors to build wealth is good business. It's also a way for banks to build lasting relevance in their communities, to reach their full potential for achieving the greatest benefit for all of their stakeholders. A kind of corporate self-actualization, if you will.

The bank I originally wrote about happens to be a faith-based financial institution that has pledged to tithe its profits to charity. But there are many ways for banks to commit to helping the communities they serve. I'm neither promoting nor detracting from those with a Christian mission. What I am suggesting is that every financial institution find its higher purpose—and follow up on that with consistent action. If a corporation is to be treated as a "person" in the eyes of the law, why not be a good one? If employees want purpose in their work, why don't you give it to them? If your community has a need that your institution can uniquely fill, why don't you fill it? Here's how one bank did it.

∞

Banking for Good

December 17, 2019

https://www.jeff4banks.com/2019/12/banking-for-good.html

It happened. A client, a bank I owned shares in, and one that I admired announced they were selling to a nearby financial institution. In June, Stewardship Financial Corporation, and their banking subsidiary, Atlantic Stewardship Bank (ASB) announced their sale to Columbia Financial Inc. (MHC) and their banking subsidiary, Columbia Bank.

It's not that I'm selfish about losing a client. Although I wished it wasn't true. What brought me down more was such a unique bank was leaving us. One that pledged 10% of its pretax profits to charity. They embraced the Old Testament tradition of tithing. In 2018, ASB tithed over $900 thousand.

From their 2018 annual report:

"From the beginning, we have been unique among American banks, founded on the Old Testament concept of stewardship. Stewardship comprises four basic tenets: ownership, responsibility, accountability and reward. We have been maintaining these ideals since our origin in 1985, particularly regarding "reward," as we tithe 10% of our annual earnings to organizations that attend to the physical, emotional and spiritual needs of others, locally and abroad. This effort includes inner-city missions, educational programs for youth, caring home environments for the elderly and spreading the Gospel. To date, we have given back over $10.1 million."

- Paul Van Ostenbridge, former President & CEO, and Michael Westra, former Chairman of the Board, Stewardship Financial Corporation

Not that Columbia Bank isn't going to pick up the mantle. When they did their first step conversion, they set up a charitable foundation, as many do when they convert from mutual to stockholder owned. The foundation pledged over $3 million last year. And as part of the ASB merger, the foundation will commit at least $500,000 per year to ASB markets. So the giving will continue.

But does this mean that a publicly traded bank, or any company, will struggle to create and honor such a pledge in the future? Nine hundred thousand dollars was over 4% of ASB's total operating expense in 2018. That means they needed 4% less somewhere else to deliver the same profits as other financial institutions. Could it have been too much of a burden to deliver the same level of profits and have the same market valuations? I realize that other banks give time and treasure to support their communities. But at ASB's level and with a public pledge to do so?

Are There Others?

There are likely others like ASB, although only one comes to mind. Providence Bank and Trust in South Holland, Illinois also pledged to tithe since its founding in 2004. Providence is now over $1 billion in total assets due to both organic and acquisition growth, and is generating solid profits. In 2018, they gave over $600 thousand to charity. The difference between Providence and ASB is that Providence is not yet public.

Is it possible to be public and to tithe?

I hope so. Because it is the natural evolution of a mixed economy that tilts more heavily towards capitalism than socialism. In a heavily socialist leaning economy, people look to government for charity. And the government looks to their people and companies to fund such charity. Eventually, the government runs out of other peoples' money.

Capitalist economies tend to generate greater innovation, efficiencies, and profit. Our public companies, in considering communities as a constituency on par with shareholders, should be able to apportion a piece of the outsized profits that a for-profit company in a capitalist economy should generate. "It is more blessed to give than to receive."

We need more Providence and Atlantic Stewardship banks.

Because we are all in this life together.

Merry Christmas everyone!

~ Jeff

∞

Since writing that article, I've become aware of Open Bank, a similar financial institution in Los Angeles. The bank's vision and mission, as articulated on its website:

To be known as a Faith-based Community Bank focused on relationship banking.

O-Our Customers: Deliver best in class client relationship management.

P-Principals: Deliver top tier shareholder returns among peer banks.

E-Employees: Become an employer of choice among employees.

N-Neighbors: Support the enhancement of our neighbors' quality of life.[xlii]

At the time of writing, OP Bancorp, the holding company for Open Bank, had a 1.51 percent ROA and a 12.42 percent ROE in its most recent year. Superior performance did not suffer, even though the bank gives away 10 percent of its pre-tax profit.

We can assume that not all boards would think tithing is right for their bank. But having a coordinated, company-wide effort to elevate the common good or battle some social plight is good strategy for any institution. It's consistent with the need to serve all of the institution's stakeholders. And that includes shareholder-owned institutions.

Most recently, commercial banks with between $1 billion and $10 billion in total assets—mostly shareholder owned—had a median expense ratio (non-interest expense to average assets) of 2.64 percent. Credit unions of the same asset size range—but designated not-for-profit and not publicly traded—had an expense ratio of 3.22 percent for the same period. At the credit union median asset size of $1.8 billion for the group I measured, the extra 58 basis points equates to nearly $10.5 million of additional operating expense.

These figures are not a testimony against credit unions. Rather, they're a testimony for the value of the profit discipline typically injected into the culture of a shareholder-owned institution. Having a high level of operating discipline generates greater resources—which allows your institution to evolve from a good corporate citizen to a great one. A greater operating discipline reduces underutilized resources that can otherwise be spread to your stakeholders. If you don't have shareholders holding your institution accountable for operating discipline, hold yourself accountable. Accomplishing your higher purpose most likely depends on it.

Aligning Your Stakeholders

How do you get everyone on board with your institution's higher purpose? That depends. Are you aiming to be an innovation enabler? A local business booster? A facilitator of economic mobility? Or is your contribution to the common good geared more toward community outreach supporting, say, sports or the arts?

It always helps to have a higher purpose that's easily identified with a financial institution. That's because your different stakeholders—employees, customers, shareholders, and communities—have different priorities and demands. I'm not convinced your institution's best intentions can take root for the long term unless you find a way to bring these stakeholders into alignment. Without alignment, your mission could become a zero-sum game, with some stakeholders winning out over others. But it doesn't need to be that way.

As much as I admire Stewardship, Providence, and Open Bank, it must be difficult to align their stakeholders. Open Bank focuses on the Korean immigrant community in Southern California. South Korea is only one-third Christian. Are the bank's employees and customers significantly different? If so, that might explain why the bank's OPEN acronym focuses on serving its stakeholders versus anything relating to religion.

Conversely, Bombas, a direct sock retailer, was founded on the philosophy of donating socks to those in need. You buy a pair of socks from them, they donate a pair to a shelter. Did you know socks are the number one item requested by homeless shelters? Bombas has evolved to include other clothing—and the more they sell, the more they donate. This company exists to help support the homeless community and bring awareness to an under-publicized problem. So far, Bombas has donated more than 43 million clothing items. The company's higher purpose is directly related to its business model, allowing it to make a maximum impact.

To be clear, I am all in on the idea that community banks should help community organizations. Years ago, I saw these words on a placard hanging on a boardroom wall: "We don't buy stadium naming rights. We're a community bank, we support the local Little League scoreboard." …Or something close to that. And I still think that community financial institutions should continue to sponsor the local Little Leagues, booster clubs, and the charity 5ks. But to make the biggest possible impact, we need to think about what banks can provide that other businesses can't.

Where can a financial institution make an impact and align its stakeholders? There is no shortage of opportunity: Elevate the economic mobility of customers through financial literacy, job creation and wage growth in your communities. Improve housing stock and neighborhood vitality through block-by-block redevelopment. Help entrepreneurs achieve business success. Provide capital for promising yet needy businesses. This list isn't exhaustive. But it does relate to the business the institution is in, the experts it has among its employees, and the needs of the community.

The SCORE Association provides a good model for how to advance small businesses—and by extension, communities. SCORE's mission is to foster vibrant small business communities through mentoring and education. Since 1964, the organization has helped more than 11 million entrepreneurs. Why don't community financial institutions do this? Imagine the difference that could be made by the

5,000 community banks across the nation if they all focused on their higher purpose in areas of need.

Alignment in Action

What does it look like when your stakeholders are aligned with your institution's higher purpose? Consider, for example, a commercial bank committed to growing the next generation of employers within its communities. How would that focus translate to the skill sets of the bank's employees, the customers it seeks, and the community support it provides?

Toward that purpose, the bank's strategy could include the following strategic objectives:

❖ Build a small business lending platform that gets to a "yes."

❖ Develop two business banking niches where there is enough opportunity in and around the bank's markets.

❖ Help those businesses in and around the bank's markets that have the greatest chance to become significant employers.

That last strategic objective could easily drift into the "doing good" aspect of this bank's higher purpose. These are businesses that might be small at first—and as such, not particularly profitable to the bank. The businesses might be capital intensive, and the founders might not have much equity. In bankers' parlance, they might not be "bankable." What's a bank supposed to do with such businesses? Give SCORE a call and pass them off to an SBA lender in the next town over? Not the bank with a higher purpose.

That bank might have an equity angel fund in its holding company, charged with investing in promising businesses that support employment growth within the bank's communities. The bank wouldn't have to inject all the funding. It could solicit other investors for the fund, and manage it. Think Shark Tank—the TV show where promising businesses pitch to a panel of venture capitalists. And the fund doesn't have to be a charity if it's run with the same operating discipline as the bank. The sharks in Shark Tank aren't doing it for charity.

The higher-purpose bank might also forge partnerships with third parties to help businesses outside of the bank's risk appetite. Companies like Fundation, for example, can broaden the population of small business customers the bank serves by using its balance sheet alongside the bank's. That allows the bank to say "yes" to more applicants, getting capital into the hands of promising businesses that it might not otherwise be willing to lend to…yet.

The higher purpose bank would likely invest in employee development, training staff to help businesses with cash flow management, accounting software, and inventory turns. Bank employees could also serve as concierges to employment agencies, government programs, and reputable local vendors to help the business get on stable footing and start to grow. Successful business owners did not all start out as good businesspeople. Bankers can fill that void and be the trusted advisor so many of their strategic plans say they are.

The higher purpose bank would focus its charitable endeavors on related initiatives, like job re-training, repurposing industrial sites, and downtown façade improvement projects. Employees would be given time to volunteer, teaching accounting basics at the local chamber of commerce or helping aspiring business owners navigate government bureaucracy.

The higher purpose bank would attract and retain purpose-driven employees. It would staff itself with people who want to build their communities by building up the businesses that operate within them. Business that employ their neighbors. It would be an institution that helps fulfill its employees' higher purpose.

This isn't altruism. It's good business. It's long-term thinking. The promising businesses you help today could be your most profitable customers tomorrow. And your employees would have helped them get there. That is alignment of your employees, customers, shareholders, and communities with your higher purpose. It is banking for good.

To Sum It Up...

Serving your stakeholders with a higher purpose need not be a zero-sum game. Dedicating resources to one constituency doesn't need to equate to reducing resources to others. Aligning your institution's higher purpose with strategy, operating discipline, accountability—and balancing it among employees, customers, shareholders, and communities—can be very rewarding to all involved. But institutions must determine their purpose, and design everything else around it.

Points Made This Chapter

❖ Banking for Good was not one of my top-read articles. But I wish it was.

❖ Capitalism is working at its peak when it reduces poverty, increases economic mobility, and provides the opportunity for people to live the way they dream of living. Banks are uniquely positioned to spur the distribution of vital capital to the community.

❖ Serving a higher purpose can equate to superior financial performance. Look at Open Bank. Shareholder-owned companies should consider the communities they serve to be as important a constituency as shareholders. And as for-profit companies in a capitalist economy, they should be able to generate outsized profits and apportion some for the benefit to the community.

❖ Having a coordinated, company-wide effort to elevate the common good or battle some social plight is good strategy for any institution. It's consistent with the need to serve all of the institution's stakeholders.

❖ Banking for good isn't altruism. It's good business.

Epilogue

*A*merican Banker, an industry go-to publication for all things banking, annually ranks the Best Banks to Work For.[xliii] The evaluation is performed by a third party that conducts extensive employee surveys and reviews employer reports on benefits and policies. Banks must opt in, but it is not a pay-to-play competition. The top 10 Best Banks to Work For had an average return on assets of 1.21 percent, almost identical to the performance of the entire industry. Being considered by your employees as the best place to work did not negatively impact financial performance.

On the contrary, it might have improved it. Many in the top 10 were very small in asset size and have not reached a scale to be able to leverage the costs inherent in banking. If you had the choice to deliver solid financial performance and be considered the best by your employees, or *not* be considered the best, which would you choose?

It is not a zero-sum game. Like Adam Smith's invisible hand, your ability to attract and retain top notch employees means you have employees looking for opportunities to improve themselves and the bank. Without executive intervention, they seek to find and destroy non value-added processes. To make the most use of technology investments. To reduce customer pain points. Top notch employees build deeper relationships and enjoy greater empowerment to make decisions that benefit both bank and customer, and hold themselves accountable and therefore motivate those around them to do the same.

Contrast that to the employee who views you as their nine-to-five. Are they asking why they do things a certain way, and search for alternatives? Are they mentoring new hires to maximize their abilities to serve the bank and its customers? Do they go the extra mile for your customers? Do they work with you or against you in creating operating discipline?

These things compound themselves. That extra expense for medical benefits, annual bonus, or paid time off would be a small down payment for the financial performance delivered by bankers who consider your bank their second family and banking as their profession.

Community building is not charity. It's survival. Think of all of those downtrodden communities that relied on one employer or one industry to sustain economic growth, only to have that employer pick up stakes and leave, or the industry flounder. Anticipate what could happen when things are good. Mobilize bank resources to prepare your communities for economic disruption, job displacement, and potential decline. Bankers are in a unique position to mitigate this risk and be part of the solution. Before a problem ever exists. Improve the net worth of your customers. Educate customers toward upward economic mobility. Support small businesses that can be the next large employers in your communities.

A key criterion for evaluating the viability of a bank stock investment is the economy in the communities where the bank operates. If the economy is moribund and trending worse, how valuable of a financial institution can you build? This requires long-term thinking, sometimes over decades. But by doing so, your financial institution can move away from just hoping the state and local government does something about your communities' decline. You can actually do something about it. Thriving communities are the seed bed for a thriving financial institution.

Hope is not a strategy. Evolve your thinking, your strategy, execution and your sense of purpose. For you, your employees, and your customers. Serve all of your stakeholders. Be an economic first responder. A squared away bank is one built to last, even when the tide goes out.

[i] Patrick McLaughlin and Oliver Sherouse, "The McLaughlin-Sherouse List: The 10 Most Regulated Industries of 2014," Mercatus Center, January 21, 2016, https://www.mercatus.org/publications/regulation/mclaughlin-sherouse-list-10-most-regulated-industries-2014.

[ii] John Mackey and Raj Sosodia, *Conscious Capitalism* (Boston: Harvard Business Review Press, 2014).

[iii] Bill Conerly, "Leadership In Today's Tight Labor Market: Reduce Employee Turnover," *Forbes*, January 19, 2018, https://www.forbes.com/sites/billconerly/2018/01/19/leadership-in-a-tight-labor-market-reduce-employee-turnover/#1bb75b7b3a6a.

[iv] Jori Epstein and Daniel Libit, "Texas Tech Women's Basketball Players Describe Toxic Culture: 'Fear, Anxiety and Depression,'" *USA Today*, August 5, 2020, https://www.usatoday.com/in-depth/sports/ncaaw/big12/2020/08/05/marlene-stollings-texas-tech-program-culture-abuse-players-say/5553370002/.

[v] Marcel Schwantes, "The Most Effective Ways to Keep Star Employees from Leaving," *Inc.*, March 15, 2017, https://www.inc.com/marcel-schwantes/first-90-days-how-to-keep-your-best-employees-from-quitting.html.

[vi] Nicholas Bloom, "How Working from Home Works Out," Stanford Institute for Economic Policy Research, June 2020, https://siepr.stanford.edu/research/publications/how-working-home-works-out.

[vii] Bloom, "How Working from Home Works Out."

[viii] Steve Greene and Jonathan Thessin, "How to Make Telework Work in a Bank," *ABA Banking Journal Podcast*, Podcast audio, December 5, 2018, https://bankingjournal.aba.com/2018/12/podcast-how-to-make-telework-work-in-a-bank/.

[ix] Lindsay McGregor and Neel Doshi, "How to Keep Your Team Motivated Remotely," *Harvard Business Review*, April 9, 2020, https://hbr.org/2020/04/how-to-keep-your-team-motivated-remotely.

ˣ "Pocket Guide for Directors," FDIC, last updated December 13, 2007, https://www.fdic.gov/regulations/resources/director/pocket/index.html.

ˣⁱ Jeff Marsico, "Banking's Top 5 in Total Return to Shareholders," *Jeff for Banks*, December 13, 2018, https://www.jeff4banks.com/2018/12/bankings-top-5-in-total-return-to.html.

ˣⁱⁱ "2019 Compensation Survey," *Bank Director*, June 2019, https://www.bankdirector.com/wp-content/uploads/2019_Compensation_Report.pdf

ˣⁱⁱⁱ "Does Gender Diversity on Boards Really Boost Company Performance?", *Knowledge@Wharton*, University of Pennsylvania, May 18, 2017, https://knowledge.wharton.upenn.edu/article/will-gender-diversity-boards-really-boost-company-performance/.

ˣⁱᵛ "Larry Fink's 2018 Letter to CEOs: A Sense of Purpose," Blackrock, Accessed January 14, 2021, https://www.blackrock.com/corporate/investor-relations/2018-larry-fink-ceo-letter.

ˣᵛ "Government and Sustainability Principles," CalPERS, Last revised September 2019, https://www.calpers.ca.gov/docs/forms-publications/governance-and-sustainability-principles.pdf.

ˣᵛⁱ Bernardo Batiz-Lazo, "A Brief History of the ATM," *The Atlantic*, March 26, 2015, https://www.theatlantic.com/technology/archive/2015/03/a-brief-history-of-the-atm/388547/.

ˣᵛⁱⁱ "Innovation and Banking: Killer Ideas or Idea Killers?", The Financial Brand, February 26, 2018, https://thefinancialbrand.com/70631/innovation-ideas-banking-culture-trends/.

ˣᵛⁱⁱⁱ Marsico, "Will Plain Vanilla Kill Community Banking?", https://www.jeff4banks.com/2011/01/will-plain-vanilla-kill-community.html.

ˣⁱˣ Marsico, "Bankers: What's Your 'Well Capitalized'?", https://www.jeff4banks.com/2015/01/bankers-whats-your-well-capitalized.html.

ˣˣ Derek McGee, "Four Ways to Deploy Excess Capital," *Bank Director Magazine*, July 23, 2018,

https://www.bankdirector.com/issues/strategy/four-ways-effectively-deploy-excess-capital/.

xxi Marsico, "Bank Dividends: Go Ahead and Drink The Kool Aid," https://www.jeff4banks.com/2017/11/bank-dividends-go-ahead-and-drink-kool.html.

xxii Robert Kafafian et al., "The Future of Community Bank Mergers," *This Month in Banking*, Podcast audio, July 24, 2018, https://kafafiangroup.com/2018/07/24/the-future-of-community-bank-mergers/.

xxiii Marsico, "Enterprise-wide Risk Management (ERM): Yawn," https://www.jeff4banks.com/2011/04/enterprise-wide-risk-management-erm.html.

xxiv Paul Davis, "Truist rising: With megamerger done, pressure on to deliver," *American Banker*, December 9, 2019, https://www.americanbanker.com/news/truist-rising-with-megamerger-done-pressure-on-to-deliver.

xxv K. Garber, "Crowded Chicago market not a factor in Byline/Ridgestone deal," *S&P Global Market Intelligence*, June 17, 2016, https://platform.marketintelligence.spglobal.com/web/client?auth=inherit#news/article?id=36854107&KeyProductLinkType=2.

xxvi "Glacier Bank Division Information," Glacier Bank, accessed January 19, 2021, https://www.glacierbank.com/about/division-information.

xxvii Kate Young, "Come Listen to a Story 'Bout Redneck Bank," *ABA Banking Journal*, April 17, 2018, https://bankingjournal.aba.com/2018/04/come-listen-to-a-story-bout-redneck-bank/.

xxviii "Flushing Financial Launches Web Bank, and a Brand," *American Banker*, November 29, 2006, https://www.americanbanker.com/news/flushing-financial-launches-web-bank-and-a-brand-ab296165.

xxix Marty Swant, "The World's Most Valuable Brands 2020," *Forbes*, https://www.forbes.com/the-worlds-most-valuable-brands/#4e117b4119c0.   At the time of original publication, the most recent Forbes ranking was "The World's Most Valuable Brands 2018."

xxx Philip Kotler, "The Importance of Branding," video by London Business Forum, posted May 20, 2020,

https://www.youtube.com/watch?v=ala1XYmWp3g.

xxxi Charles Spence et al., "Eating with our eyes: From visual hunger to digital satiation," *Brain and Cognition* 110, (December 2016): 53-63,

https://doi.org/10.1016/j.bandc.2015.08.006.

xxxii Marsico, "A Time of Reckoning for Your Bank's Core Deposits?",

https://www.jeff4banks.com/2018/03/a-time-of-reckoning-for-your-banks-core.html.

xxxiii EF Hutton, "When EF Hutton talks, people listen - 'Restaurant' commercial," YouTube video, posted March 2, 2017, https://youtu.be/2_ygqPepLjM

xxxiv John Oxford, *No More Next Time: Marketing in the Age of Distraction*, (Tupelo: Oxford Productions, LLC., 2020), Kindle edition.

xxxv Mark Gibson and Kevin Halsey, "How to Build Remarkable Products," *ABA Banking Journal*, September 15, 2017,

https://bankingjournal.aba.com/2017/09/build-remarkable-bank-products/.

xxxvi "Standards Needed for Safe, Small Installment Loans from Banks and Credit Unions," Pew Charitable Trusts, February 15, 2018,

https://www.pewtrusts.org/en/research-and-analysis/issue-briefs/2018/02/standards-needed-for-safe-small-installment-loans-from-banks-credit-unions.

xxxvii "The State of Digital Lending," American Bankers Association, January 8, 2018, https://www.aba.com/news-research/research-analysis/state-digital-lending.

xxxviii This book does not count regulators as a primary constituent because a bank that satisfies its communities, employees, customers, and shareholders might not always be aligned with what regulators would like it to do. It's worth noting, though, that as a next-level constituent, regulators are concerned with financial metrics.

Earnings is reflected by the "E" in the CAMELS rating system for classifying a bank's overall condition.

xxxix Marsico, "Branch Talk,"

https://www.jeff4banks.com/2018/06/branch-talk.html.

xl Marsico, "Too Small to Succeed in Banking,"

https://www.jeff4banks.com/2013/04/too-small-to-succeed-in-banking.html.

xli Daniel Carson, "Old Fort Bank sold to employees," *Fremont News Messenger*, January 20, 2016,

https://www.thenews-messenger.com/story/news/local/2016/01/20/old-fort-bank-sold-employees/79070576/.

xlii "Our Vision & Mission," About, Open Bank, accessed January 26, 2021

https://myopenbank.com/about/#vision-mission.

xliii Laura Alix and Jackie Steward, "Best Banks to Work For 2020," *American Banker*, October 27, 2020,

https://www.americanbanker.com/list/best-banks-to-work-for.